Sandra shares in a comprehensive way her path of healing and wellness in Christ with all its dimensions—physical, mental, spiritual, and social. Out of her deep pain and deeper faith in Jesus, we read about all she has learned as she journeyed with Christ through pain and toward a healthy, renewed, and full new life.

—Philip Mamalakis, PhD
Holy Cross Greek Orthodox School of Theology
Author, *Parenting Toward the Kingdom*

I am delighted to endorse Sandra Tadros Guirguis and her captivating memoir, which explores a profound journey of grief, healing, and spiritual growth. With an unwavering commitment to Christian values, Sandra offers invaluable insights on living well for Jesus, while emphasizing mental and physical health. Her book is a treasure trove of inspiration and guidance that glorifies God and embodies the virtues of the Christian faith. Prepare to be uplifted and transformed by Sandra's remarkable story.

—Fr. Botrous Philopos
Priest and Registered Psychotherapist

From the very start, this book was so deeply captivating and I could not put it down. It talks about the connection between nutrition and the mind, body, and soul so effortlessly, and breaks down topics in an easy-to-understand manner. I would highly recommend this insightful book that provides many lessons and wisdom.

—Christine Francis, RD, DDEPT
Owner and Registered Dietitian at Christine the RD

The lessons you share throughout the book on grief, self-care and finding joy are inspirational. Your vulnerability in speaking about how your journey of ultimately turning a tragedy into a life of purpose for you and your children is something that will provide hope to others in their darkest days of grief. It is my honour to endorse your book, Sandra. Thank you for sharing this with the world.

—Dr. Aleksandra Brankovic, MD

Embracing Abundance is a genuine, compassionate, and practical guide for anyone who has gone through grief, loss, or trauma. Sandra courageously shares her own journey of healing, offering authentic hope and heartfelt insights in addition to a step-by-step holistic approach to recovery. An easy read that is truly inspiring! I look forward to her next book.

—Dr. Michael Armanyous
Lead Psychiatrist, Shared-Care Mental Health Service,
Toronto Western Hospital
Assistant Professor, Department of Psychiatry, University of Toronto

Embracing ABUNDANCE

A Journey to Wellness and Wholeness through Faith and Self-Care

Sandra Tadros Guirguis

EMBRACING ABUNDANCE
Copyright © 2023 by Sandra Tadros Guirguis

All rights reserved. Neither this publication nor any part of this publication may be reproduced or transmitted in any form or by any means, electronic or mechanical, including photocopying, recording or any information storage and retrieval system, without permission in writing from the author.

Scripture taken from the New King James Version®. Copyright © 1982 by Thomas Nelson. Used by permission. All rights reserved. Scripture quotations marked (NIV) are taken from the Holy Bible, New International Version®, NIV®. Copyright © 1973, 1978, 1984, 2011 by Biblica, Inc.™ Used by permission of Zondervan. All rights reserved worldwide. www.zondervan.com The "NIV" and "New International Version" are trademarks registered in the United States Patent and Trademark Office by Biblica, Inc.™

The information contained in this document is intended for educational and entertainment purposes only. All effort has been executed to present accurate, up-to-date, complete, and reliable information. No warranties of any kind are declared or implied. Readers acknowledge that the author is not engaging in the rendering of legal, financial, medical, or professional advice. The content in this book has been derived from various sources. Please consult a licensed professional before attempting any techniques outlined in this book.

ISBN: 978-1-7382202-0-5
eBook ISBN: 978-1-7382202-1-2
Audio Book ISBN: 978-1-7382202-2-9

Faithful Pen Press

Cataloguing in Publication information can be obtained from Library and Archives Canada.

JESUS, I DEDICATE THIS BLANK PAGE TO YOU.
I have never previously written a book, but I feel You nudging my heart. Lord, if this is Your will for me, and if this will bring glory to You as well as help others, then I will write. Please guide my thoughts, my hands, and my steps to Your will. Amen.

ACKNOWLEDGEMENTS

I ACKNOWLEDGE WITH gratitude my Saviour, Jesus Christ. I love You and thank You for Your infinite love. May You be glorified always.

To my cherished husband, Fady. Thank you for always being my biggest supporter. Whether it's setting up lights and cameras behind the scenes, holding up my notes for me during a video (best teleprompter ever), or holding down the fort so I could spend time writing, you are always helpful. You encouraged me to write a book several years ago and continued to inspire me to do so until I finally asked the Holy Spirit to help me. And here we are! Thank you for not letting it go. God bless you.

To my beloved children—Gabe, Bella, and Ben. You fill our lives with such beauty and love. We pray that you grow into the disciples you are meant to be and that you shine Jesus's light wherever you go.

To my dearest parents and brother (and sister), you have been my biggest supporters in life. You physically and emotionally carried me as an infant and as a broken woman, when I was grieving, when I had respiratory distress, and at every other time in between. Whether it's a hug, a prayer, or a pot of Mama's wara enab (stuffed grape leaves) or Baba's salata (salad), you always serve with love.

To the beloved Tadros clan, and all the other last names included in this beautiful big family. I must also thank the Ibrahim, Guirguis, Elagizi, and Youssef families. You are all incredibly precious to me and I pray for your peace and joy always.

To my dearest friends, my Walking with Jesus and Surrender Sister groups, my colleagues, my priests, my church groups, and all my other communities, you humble me with your encouragement and support. Life is so much richer with you in it.

To our precious angel, Mina. You lived your life as the most wonderful example of Christ-like love. You will never be forgotten. Heaven gained a most wonderful angel when you returned home. May you always rest in wonderful peace.

To my dedicated publishing team—Jen and Evan—thank you for your faith-focused expertise and dedication. Your contributions enriched the journey of sharing this message with the world.

Contents

ACKNOWLEDGEMENTS	VII
INTRODUCTION	XI
One: **IDENTITY**	1
Two: **RESOURCES AND GRIEF SUPPORT**	5
Three: **CHILDREN**	13
Four: **UNDERSTANDING WELLNESS**	17
Five: **STRESS AND WELLNESS**	29
Six: **RELATIONSHIPS AND WELLNESS**	33
Seven: **MEDITATION AND MINDFULNESS**	37
Eight: **EXERCISE**	45
Nine: **NUTRITION**	55
Ten: **GUT MICROBIOME**	65
Eleven: **SELF-CARE**	69
Twelve: **SINGING AND LAUGHING**	75
Thirteen: **GIVE**	79
Fourteen: **SLEEP**	83
Fifteen: **HEALING AND TRIGGERS**	87
Sixteen: **FORMER IN-LAWS**	93
Seventeen: **MOVING FORWARD**	95
Eighteen: **DATING**	97
Nineteen: **HOW TO KNOW IF SOMETHING COMES FROM JESUS**	103
CONCLUSION	107
ABOUT THE AUTHOR	109

INTRODUCTION

HAVE YOU EVER sat amidst the ashes of your life in bewildered horror, looked up to the God you've served so faithfully, and screamed "Why, God, why? You're all-powerful! Why didn't you stop this tragedy?"

I hug you, I pray for you, and I can relate to you. In my case, it was grief after the death of a loved one. For others, it may be divorce, abuse, or another form of life-altering trauma. I am sorry for your pain.

The goal of this book is to share my journey with you, in the hopes that you'll feel some comfort in knowing that someone else has navigated this difficult road that lies ahead of you, that there are others who are reaching a hand back to help you through your pain and perhaps fear of the unknown. I'll share what worked for me as well as the resources and tools I've found most helpful. I'll share how Jesus carried me through. I want to tell you that you can heal from this and create a new life for yourself, one that includes joy and laughter.

It may seem impossible right now, but have hope, dear friend. Jesus wants you to live your life to the fullest, even if it's not the life you ever envisioned or wanted. It will be different yet beautiful. You are not alone.

I am passionate about mental and physical well-being, and I love Jesus and give full glory to Him for anything and everything that has happened in my life. If you would like to join me, we'll walk together and discuss all the items that helped me through my grief. This includes my Christian faith as well as specific strategies to improve my mental health, gut health, sleep, and exercise habits.

Before the Loss

I see an element of naivety when I reflect back to the time in my life before tragedy struck. I can see myself as Sandra-before (or Sandra 1.0) and then Sandra-after (or Sandra 2.0). Without a doubt, I was shattered. With God's grace, I am whole now but changed.

Unfortunately for those closest to me, one thing that didn't change was my penchant for cheesy and nerdy jokes!

Sandra 1.0 had the confidence of someone who was secure in her identity and whose life plan was proceeding exactly on track. I had studied hard and was working in my profession of choice. I was married to a wonderful man who shared the same values and faith as I did. We had built a beautiful home and family together and I was expecting our first child after a long struggle with fertility treatments. I had held my breath until we passed that first trimester and was joyfully awaiting our first child. I could cheerfully envision our lives five, ten, and twenty years ahead. My husband and I often had chatted about our short- and long-term goals. Since I have a type-A personality, I often took great joy in setting goals, making lists, and then crushing them.

The Loss

My husband had started experiencing some health struggles, but it was nothing to worry about too much, as far as we were told. He had routine surgery to remove his spleen just before our daughter was born and was supposed to be on his feet again within a few weeks. There would be time to spare before the delivery. Recovery was going to take four to six weeks and then he would resume work and all his regular activities.

This is not how things went.

INTRODUCTION

From almost the minute he emerged from surgery, the situation went from bad to worse. My husband endured a lot of mysterious and unforeseen complications, ICU visits, a rare blood transfusion reaction, as well as organ failure. He was in a lot of pain and suffered greatly. The doctors suspected he might have some type of underlying inflammatory condition, but none of their tests were ever conclusive.

His condition was extremely critical, and several times during his hospital admission our priests came to pray for him and give him Holy Communion. We were grateful for the family and friends who held a constant and rotating vigil. They brought food, lots of water, prayers, and icons.

I was nine months pregnant and spending nights on an uncomfortable chair that could barely contain me. Neither my husband nor I had a peaceful night's rest for the months leading up to the birth of our first child.

If you've ever tried to sleep in a hospital, you'll know that there's a constant influx of healthcare providers coming around to assess or medicate the patient. There's certainly no shortage of beeping machines. Let's not forget the heart-breaking soundtrack of other patients or their families sobbing or speaking too loudly.

When I went into labour, it was completely different from how I had envisioned it. We had previously toured the hospital and I remember almost skipping down the halls as I pictured my husband and I arriving on that fateful day, overjoyed. I would have my cute overnight bag. There would be smiles all around when it was time to deliver my daughter.

My husband remained in ICU at the downtown hospital while I went to a different hospital to give birth. I was so worried about my husband, and also so worried about labour. The two fears seemed to play off each other.

God has not given you a spirit of fear, I kept reminding myself.

I tried my best to calm my breathing and focus on the moment. It was so challenging.

My delivery was tough. I tried my playlist, the whirlpool, and my maternity breathing, but nothing seemed to help. Yet when they laid my daughter on my chest for skin-to-skin contact, it was one of the most incredible moments of my life. I couldn't believe that after all the prayers and fertility treatments my prayers had been answered.

I just wished my husband could have been there too.

We fasted, we prayed, and after several months he was able to come home! It was a miracle! We yelled, "God is so good!"

He needed home and wound care, a walker, and other supplies—but the important thing was that he lived! Life was a bit difficult with a new baby and his recovery, but we were over the moon to be together again. After his hospitalization, he had new issues with his heart and kidneys, requiring dialysis, and occasionally he also needed home oxygen.

As a healthcare provider, I had vaguely heard of the baby blues, but it was another thing entirely to experience it for myself. I was so happy to have my baby and my husband home, but I also felt deeply exhausted. I would carry my husband's walker out of the car, followed by the baby seat, and alternate between his appointments and her appointments. Afterward I would go home and cry in the shower.

The situation gradually improved over time and I felt grateful that this illness, this rocky patch, was behind us.

Or so I thought.

Two years later, we had a second child and just couldn't believe how blessed we were with our beautiful baby boy. All the while, my husband was healing and getting stronger.

However, two years after the birth of our second child my husband became ill again. At first, it manifested as a routine cold. We were always a little worried about his health, but not significantly so since this time he was talking and laughing and his vitals were good.

When he didn't improve as quickly as expected, we headed to the hospital just to be thorough.

The children and I stayed with him in the examination room. The doctors expected to monitor him for a day or two before sending him home. He and I chatted for a bit, and then I decided to head out to take the kids for some fresh air. Some other family members stayed with him.

Suddenly, I got a call from his family that he had been rushed to the ICU.

My heart hammering, I dropped the kids off with my parents and rushed back to the hospital.

We've been here before, I told myself. *Everything's going to be okay.*

But it was never again okay. When I'd spoken to him earlier in the examination room, I'd had no idea that was the last time I would ever speak to him. I wish I had said something more profound, or that I could recall it a bit better.

His infection worsened in the ICU and he was kept sedated. I sat for hours beside his bed, talking to him and praying over him. His head would turn at the sound of my voice and I believe that he could hear me. I talked and talked and talked.

Again, everyone frantically prayed. Our family and church friends visited with a shroud, an icon, and holy oil. We placed these items on him and under his pillow. In addition to prayer, we held vigils and we fasted. We were confident that our all-powerful and compassionate God would not take away this wonderful human who was a beloved son, brother, cousin, husband, father, compassionate physician and man of faith. No way. It just wasn't going to happen. It couldn't.

It happened.

> God doesn't promise that there won't be hardships in this life. However, He does promise that He will never give us more than we can endure, although I must say that I felt very alone for a long time.

I later recalled that God doesn't promise that there won't be hardships in this life. However, He does promise that He will never give us more than we can endure, although I must say that I felt very alone for a long time.

It happened so fast and in slow motion at the same time. I saw the nurse's mounting panic as the telemetry machine kept sounding the alarm, despite all her efforts to add more medication to the IV.

Once the code blue was paged, a stampede of scrub-clad bodies rushed past me in a frenzy of quick yet controlled movements. It might have been one minute or one hour that they worked on him. I don't know. All I know is that what followed was the loudest silence I have ever heard.

"Cause of death: septic shock. Time of death: 10:16 a.m."

I stared at the ICU doctor, willing him to retract those awful words. My mind kept screaming, *No! He's wrong! There's been some mistake!*

I mumbled incoherently while sobbing over my husband, thinking that this must be a nightmare. Only one thing comforted me in that moment: I looked at his face, really looked, and noticed how incredibly peaceful he seemed. When you're in pain, you don't always realize it, but the pain is etched into the lines of the face.

All that was gone.

What I didn't yet know was that at 10:16 that morning, I died too. The only difference is that I was still walking around—a shell of my former self.

After the Loss

It was easy to stay numb and in denial those first few days. I went home and had to quickly go through the closet to pick out clothing for him to wear at his funeral. How awful is that? I'm grateful for my family, who helped me and drove with me to the funeral home. There were so many questions to answer and details to settle. I just sat there, nodding dumbly and dabbing at my eyes in a surreal sort of bewilderment. At one point I remember calmly following the funeral home employee into a side room to select a casket, seeing rows upon rows of caskets, and realizing that my husband was going to be buried in one…

It was too much. I ran screaming and fortunately someone else from the family was able to make that decision for me.

Plans were quickly made for the viewing and funeral, but I remained hyper-focused on how I would tell my children. This was going to crush them. What should I say? How would anything be okay again? How could I help them when I myself could barely function?

Until this point in my life, prayer had always helped. Right now, however, I was incredibly angry with God. I felt completely betrayed. I had cut my teeth on stories of miracles from the Bible. It would have been *so* easy for Jesus to heal my husband. I had asked every saint, every archangel, to intercede for us. How could God not have spared us this pain?

I did, however, feel the prayers of those around me. And I believe that God did send me the lovely social worker who came to speak with me. She advised me to tell the children that my husband had died and to be as clear about it as possible. She also gave me the idea to have a private viewing for just the children. This would provide them with some closure and an opportunity to say goodbye and leave a letter or trinkets in the coffin.

I was still anxious about telling them, though. The words I used would change their lives forever.

Delivering such painful news, breaking the hearts of my children, was one of the worst things I ever had to endure.

My two-year-old son didn't quite understand what I was saying, and he kept asking heartbreakingly sweet questions like "So how do we visit in heaven?" and "When is he coming home from heaven?"

But my daughter understood it as well as an adult, although she still had the emotions of a four-year-old. The news was too much for her little heart to bear. There was a moment or two of stillness, a calm before the storm, and then the full impact of my words hit. The devastation was catastrophic. You never, ever forget the sounds and accompanying chills of an adult cry of agony being ripped from the throat of your four-year-old daughter.

At our private viewing, I'll never forget standing behind my children as they walked up to the casket, their little bodies barely taller than the casket itself, and said, "Bye, Dad. See you in heaven" and "I made you a picture."

The first few weeks in the life of Sandra 2.0 went by in a miserable blur. Dead Sandra loved being busy. It kept her unwanted thoughts and feelings at bay.

I had received a checklist from the people at the funeral home, and it included all the things I needed to do to resolve my husband's affairs, such as cancelling his health card and passport. As I've mentioned, I love making lists—and I attacked this one with vigour.

In the aftermath of my husband's death, I kept my kids busy and exercised until it took the edge off my building hysteria. Every day was like Groundhog Day. Rinse and repeat.

It might have seemed like I was doing well to the people around me, but appearances can be deceptive. At times, I even deceived myself.

One of my favourite books is called *The Body Keeps the Score* by Bessel van der Kolk. In it, he writes about the physical effects that result from trauma. Later in this book, we will revisit the body's warning signs pertaining to stress and how to manage them.

Initially I tried to outrun my grief. The challenge, though, is that it always catches up, and often at inopportune times. Once while strolling through the grocery store, I heard a familiar song come over the speakers, an old song by Stevie Nicks. The lyrics punched me right in the stomach. The reaction was so unexpected and intense that I rushed my cart behind one of the freezers, crouched down, and bawled my eyes out. That was uncomfortable. It was a beautiful song with happy memories tied to it. My reaction was visceral.

Another time, while waiting in line at the coffee shop to order my favourite decaf latte, I heard the person in front of me order a pumpkin spice latte. Just like that, a rush of memories assaulted me and I had to run to my car before the onslaught of tears came.

Additionally, my husband was a devoted fan of the Kansas City Chiefs, even though they hadn't made it to the super bowl in many years. After he passed, they finally made it to the Super Bowl. It was tough not having him around to celebrate their success. However, thinking about him enjoying a heavenly Super Bowl party brought some comfort.

I eventually allowed myself short periods of time every few days just to sit with my grief. I didn't try to rush or fix the grief; I just acknowledged it—and that helped.

I will be forever grateful to everyone who sent me messages and Bible verses. Although I didn't answer the phone during this time or reply to many messages, I eventually compiled them. When I was ready to read them, they provided incredible comfort.

I'll also be forever grateful to everyone who dropped off food, gift cards, or activities for the children. I have to thank my family and friends. Even though they were hurting too, they did their best to support us. May God reward you all a million times over.

As time went on, I kept praying. I told God that I was still mad but really needed some help. I prayed over my children repeatedly and asked for guidance and discernment. I began to read encouraging passages from the Bible.

Although I didn't believe things would ever be okay again, I still found comfort in Jeremiah 29:11: *"'For I know the plans I have for you,' declares the Lord, 'plans to prosper you and not to harm you, plans to give you hope and a future'"* (NIV). I really wanted to believe I could hope for a good future, but I just couldn't imagine it. Every day felt like crawling over broken glass.

STUDY GUIDE QUESTIONS

1. Have you ever felt like God abandoned you during a period of your life?

2. During this time, how did you reconcile with God in your heart? What passages of Scripture or comforting thoughts helped you?

One

IDENTITY

ONE OF THE first big hurdles I faced was struggling with my new identity. Now, if I were to ask you to tell me who you are in a few words, what would you say? Think about it for a moment. The words that come to mind may be the ones you most strongly associate with your identity. You might respond with your profession, your accomplishments, or your family status.

What was my new identity? I had to come to terms with the fact that I was now a *widow*. I felt lost on many levels. My days looked different, my heart hurt all the time, and I didn't know what to do with myself. For someone like me, who'd always had a plan, this was so disconcerting.

While filling out a form at the dentist one day, I came to the section relating to my marital status. I almost checked off *married* automatically, as I had done for so many years. But then I paused and hovered over the word *widow*. As I stared at that five-letter word, I felt like it jumped off the page and slapped me.

That word hurt me so much.

Our feelings are often the result of our previous knowledge and experience. Well, when I thought about what a widow looks like, I thought of a helpless woman, outcast from society as in the older days. I pictured someone much older than I was, someone who was resigned to wearing black all her days and just tolerating life until she too went to heaven.

There was something very sad and heart-breaking about this image that surfaced in my mind. I balked at claiming that word as my own.

Nevertheless, I checked off *widow* on the form and sat down, uncomfortably waiting for the dental hygienist to call me in.

The word kept clanging in my brain. Widow. Did that describe me? What did it mean? I didn't want to be a widow. I didn't want to have lost my husband. I had planned on us growing old and raising our children together. The intention was for us to live a long, happy life together. We had prayed, gone to church, and tried to live a healthy lifestyle. None of this was supposed to have happened...

I once read that some of the biggest struggles we face come about when our expectations don't align with our reality. I find this to be true, both professionally and personally. I really resisted my new reality, and it was some time before I was able to form a new identity for myself, by the grace of God. I didn't want to become a professional widow, nor did I want to continue living like a half-person, someone who had literally and painfully lost the other half of herself.

I tried to lean into God like never before. It was difficult, because I continued to feel angry with Him. I was so disappointed that He had let me down.

My True Identity

While studying Colossians in a Bible study with a group of friends—we call ourselves the Surrender Sisters, hoping to surrender to the Lord always—one of them remarked on something so beautiful in the epistle's introduction that I had completely missed.

In the first line, Paul did not identify himself as Paul the Philosopher or Paul the Preacher. Instead he identified himself as Paul the Apostle of Jesus Christ. How incredible! I decided that I wanted to focus on my identity as Sandra, belonging to Christ.

I continued to remind myself that He loves me. Not only that, but He loves my late husband and my children even more than I love

ONE: IDENTITY

them, which is a tremendous amount. That day, I made the conscious choice to trust Him to help us.

STUDY GUIDE QUESTIONS

1. If you had to describe yourself in one word, what would it be? Why does this word identify you?

2. Look through the Bible and find how God describes you. Some good examples include Ephesians 2:10, Psalm 139:14, John 15:9, and Ephesians 1:4.

Two

RESOURCES AND GRIEF SUPPORT

WHEN IT COMES to grief, it's important to acknowledge and share your pain. I've noticed that people are sometimes reluctant to share their pain in group sessions because they feel as though their loss isn't as tragic or doesn't rank as "bad" as someone else's. Sometimes in group therapy one person might share something devastating and the next person who speaks will preface their story with a qualifier, such as "What I went through isn't as bad as what she went through…"

I want to halt that thought right away. If you're holding back because of a comparison you're making, remember that there is no hierarchy when it comes to the intensity of pain and loss. Only you truly understand the depth of your own pain.

It's important to embrace your grief journey fully and seek the support you need. Remember that seeking help is a courageous and crucial step towards healing.

The Grieving Process
The Mayo Clinic states that different people follow different paths through the grieving experience. The order and timing of these phases may vary from person to person:

- Accepting the reality of your loss
- Allowing yourself to experience the pain of your loss[1]

---

[1] I struggled hard with this one.

- Adjusting to a new reality in which the deceased is no longer present
- Having other relationships[2]

It can be reassuring to understand that the grief cycle has five stages—denial, bargaining, anger, depression, and acceptance—and that they are fluid, meaning that you can flow back and forth between the stages until you finally reach acceptance.[3]

I once read a study which stated that more than half of survivors report struggling to find resources for grief. I can believe that, and I imagine that the actual percentage is much higher.

Why Do Bad Things Happen to Good People?

This is a question I pondered often. I would ask God, *Why take such a good person so early in his life, Lord?*

The book of Job deals with the issue of why God allows bad things to happen to good people. Job was a righteous man, yet he suffered in ways that are almost beyond belief. God allowed the evil one to inflict all kinds of pain and torment on Job, although he couldn't kill him. Still, he did his worst.

Through it all, Job's response was incredible:

> Though He slay me, yet will I trust Him. Even so, I will defend my own ways before Him. (Job 13:15)
>
> The Lord gave, and the Lord has taken away; blessed be the name of the Lord. (Job 1:21)

Job chose to focus on knowing that God was good, trusting Him even if he couldn't make any sense of the suffering. I continue to find his example incredibly inspiring.

---

[2] "Complicated Grief," *Mayo Clinic*. December 13, 2022 (https://www.mayoclinic.org/diseases-conditions/complicated-grief/symptoms-causes/syc-20360374).

[3] The grief cycle was first introduced by Dr. Elisabeth Kübler-Ross in her 1969 book, *On Death and Dying* (New York, NY: Scribner, 1997).

The Resources that Supported Me

I want to share the various resources that I personally found helpful, and through doing so encourage you to have hope. Your life doesn't need to remain in a frozen state of autopilot. You don't need to feel dead inside and robotic. You can choose to live—and live abundantly.

A turning point for me came when I read a devotional from Proverbs 31 Ministries, the name being a reference to the godly woman described in Proverbs 31. On the ministry's website, women collectively write encouraging blogs and support each other. I visited this site some days, and other days I didn't, but I'm so grateful to have read this one particular devotional. I thank God for nudging me to do so.

The author, Tracie Miles, had written of her pain over her marital breakdown:

> Life as I knew it had ended, and I had a choice to make. I could either let my circumstances dictate my joy and happiness going forward, or I could intentionally choose to be positive and refuse to sink under the weight of negativity…
>
> With each passing day, I felt the toxicity of negativity, hopelessness, fear, and pessimism seeping deeper into my heart…
>
> My heart lightened when I surrendered my negativity and committed to trusting God through this storm…
>
> A positive mind will lead to a positive life, even when life is hard. God has a positive life waiting for you. All you have to do is embrace it, and open the door for transformation, one positive thought at a time.[4]

---

[4] Tracie Miles, "How to Life a Life of Optimism After Divorce," *Crosswalk*. April 30, 2019 (https://www.crosswalk.com/family/marriage/divorce-and-remarriage/how-to-live-a-life-of-optimism-after-divorce.html).

I must thank Proverbs 31 for their beautiful ministry. Those words impacted me more than they could have known.

Next I want to share about another resource, quite unexpected, that helped me move out of my frozen state.

But first, let me ask you an important question. Do you believe in miracles? Do you believe that God sends people to help right when you need it? Does He send encouragement on a bad day?

For me, the answer is yes.

> Do you believe in miracles? Do you believe that God sends people to help right when you need it? Does He send encouragement on a bad day?
> For me, the answer is yes.

Years ago, I lost touch with a childhood friend from high school. She was always a lovely person and dear to me, but we drifted apart and didn't see each other for a long time. But when she heard about my loss, she came to the funeral service and offered love and support.

She had a sister who I knew from having visited their home during high school. This sister was saddened to hear what had happened to me and decided to mail me a book. This didn't turn out to be just any book but rather one that gave me the practical steps and encouragement I needed in order to move out of my numb state and truly live again. Reading this book, I encountered the story of another young widow with young children. As I read it, I kept nodding my head vigorously and saying "Yes! Me too! Exactly!" It is beautifully written and includes practical and easy-to-follow activities and suggestions.

After receiving it in the mail, however, I didn't read it at first. It came a few weeks after the funeral and I was touched by the gesture. However, Sandra 2.0 had such brain fog and fatigue during this period that I could only read a few lines at a time. Even then, I found myself having to reread them because I just couldn't focus.

TWO: RESOURCES AND GRIEF SUPPORT

Sandra 1.0 had devoured books with a voracious appetite, so this was a big adjustment for me.

So I opened the book, but I eventually parked it. Only when I picked it up again did it rock my world in the best way. It was so empowering for me to read about someone else who had gone through the same experiences and not only survived but managed to have a happy life in which she fully laughed and loved again. Wow![5]

By the time I finished the book, I was so inspired and encouraged. I started taking chances socially again. Something was changing inside me. From the bottom of my heart, I am thankful for receiving this book when I did.

It can be difficult to find resources. Here are some other resources you may connect with as you need support.

Your primary healthcare provider. After a traumatic experience, there is an increased risk of substance abuse and self-harm. If you are going through trauma, you are encouraged to touch base regularly with your healthcare provider, counsellor, or other trusted professional. Any thoughts of self-harm or harm to others should be considered a medical emergency that requires immediate attention. Please familiarize yourself with a twenty-four-hour crisis line phone number in your area.

Community. Years ago, I attended a two-day Applied Suicide Intervention Skills Training (ASIST) with my colleagues. The workshop provided valuable training. The goal was to teach participants how to minimize the risk of suicide by recognizing its signs, providing a skilled intervention, and developing a safety plan for someone in distress. To the workers who take these calls daily, may God fortify, strengthen, and bless you.

---

[5] Christina Rasmussen, *Second Firsts: Learn to Live, Love, and Laugh Again* (Carlsbad, CA: Hay House Publisher, 2013). The truth is that I have since learned that this author writes and speaks on some subjects which don't align with my Christian perspective, so I can't wholeheartedly recommend her. This book did, however, greatly impact me for the better.

During the ASIST training, we did some role-playing to anticipate how the conversation might go. We learned that it can be helpful to try identifying protective factors during the conversation. One of the biggest protective factors is community. Feeling connected to others in a school, in a place of worship, on a sports team, or other community setting is very important.

Grief groups and counsellors. During my recovery, I learned a lot about grief resources. There are support groups in the community, offered by the province, offered privately, and offered as part of hospice care. There are groups that address loss in a generalized sense as well as more specialized groups that deal with the experiences of losing a parent, spouse, or child. There are also drop-in sessions and closed sessions.

Counsellors and grief centres are available where children can draw a picture about how they feel, light a candle, or use physical activity to work through their emotions. Sometimes you will need to try a few different groups or activities before finding the one that really fits with you. It can take time to find someone with whom you can talk openly and comfortably to help you navigate this difficult time.

For articles on pain and loss from a Christian perspective, I recommend visiting the website of Focus on the Family.

Supporting others. In the year after my husband passed away, friends told me about another young woman with young children who had just lost her husband. I was incredibly sad to hear this and could really feel her pain. They asked if it would be okay for them to connect us, since she had heard about me and discovered I'd lived through a similar experience. I readily agreed and was happy to help.

However, I was also nervous. I was hanging onto life by a thread myself and never knew when a grief curve ball would hit me. How could I help her?

In any case, I agreed to meet with her.

We met at a coffee shop and hugged like we had known each other forever, although of course we had only just met. Our eyes watered simultaneously and we had a shared understanding as survivors who'd been left adrift in this world.

We talked and talked. We talked about how we felt as well as discussed all the little things that had become so difficult, such as sleeping on your side of the bed and still thinking of the other side as your husband's side even though he wasn't coming back.

Some parts of the conversation really challenged me. For example, she asked me when things were going to get better and I had to tell her, honestly, that I didn't have an answer. Certainly the answer would be different for everyone.

At the end of the conversation, she told me that she felt significantly better and asked if we could keep in touch. We certainly did remain in contact.

I learned something very important that day: you don't have to have all of the answers, or any of them, to help another person who's struggling. In this case, authentically sharing with another person to whom I could relate was incredibly helpful—to both of us.

A few months later, I was introduced to another young widow, and then another, and then yet another. I became a sort of "widow whisperer" in the community, someone who was called upon any time a woman was widowed and wanted to chat with someone who had been through the same thing.

In fact, that's the reason I have ultimately written this book. I have no idea whether this book will be helpful, but I keep writing— and reliving uncomfortable times—because of the feeling in my heart that God wants me to reach out to others. When I pray, I feel God's affirmations about it.

If even one person, just one, feels even marginally better and more supported after reading this book, I will be overjoyed. That will make the long writing process worthwhile.

When I told my parents that I was working on this book, in fact, my dad sent me an encouraging text. I saved and have prayed it almost daily. He wrote, "May the Holy Spirit talk through this book for the edification, comfort, and joy of all God's children." Amen!

STUDY GUIDE QUESTIONS

1. What are the four phases of the grieving experience, according to the Mayo Clinic?

2. Have you ever experienced what you felt was a little miracle of God? Perhaps when you were sent the right resource or person exactly when you needed it?

Three

CHILDREN

I WAS INCREDIBLY worried about my children and spoke about them to every mental health provider I came across, which were many since I work in the healthcare field. I was repeatedly told that children are resilient and will heal with time and support. I wanted to believe that with every fibre in my body.

In my humble opinion, getting professional help is always a good idea. After the funeral, when I was trying to secure the best resources for my children, we were invited to a child's birthday party at an indoor playground. I jumped at the chance to go somewhere fun with the kids!

While they climbed around the play structures, the parents stood around chatting. The parents hosting the party were both lovely friends of mine whom I'd grown up with. Another adult there was the best friend of the dad, and he introduced me to his sister, who was visiting from out of town. We got to chatting and it turned out she was a grief counsellor.

Another miracle? I always thought it was.

She shared with me something so valuable, something that I've shared with many other parents since. She said that kids want to know four things, whether or not they can articulate them. These are the four C's of grief:

> Kids want to know four things, whether or not they can articulate them. These are the four C's of grief.

- Can I catch it?
- Did I cause it?
- Can I cure it?
- Who will care for me?[6]

I found these questions to be so interesting and important. I made a mental note to discuss them with my children.

After we got home that afternoon and they tore through their loot bags, full of goodies, we sat down and I broached these questions.

"You know you didn't cause what happened to Daddy, right guys?" I began.

To my surprise, my daughter turned to me with her eyes wide. "We didn't?" she asked in earnest hope. "Are you sure?"

I was taken aback by this question. Never in a million years had I imagined that she somehow thought she or her brother were the cause of her dad's illness. I sat there, feeling both stunned and immensely grateful for these questions.

I asked my daughter to clarify why she thought she may have caused the illness. She explained.

One day, many months ago, he had come home from dialysis feeling weak, but she and her brother had run to hug him. She had been harbouring guilt and fear that they had somehow harmed him and it eventually led to his passing.

We clarified in detail and at length what had caused his death and confirmed that it had nothing to do with anything they had done. There hadn't been any cure available and his illness hadn't been contagious.

Lastly, we came to the question of who would care for them now that their father was gone. This was important to them. Prior to his death, I don't think either of them could even have fathomed that a parent would die. We were invincible to them.

---

[6] "What are the 4 C's?" *KidsGrief.ca*. Date of access: June 21, 2023 (https://kidsgrief.ca/mod/lesson/view.php?id=261).

THREE: CHILDREN

Now they had seen firsthand that death could happen, leading them to fear what would happen if their mom were to die too. So we discussed wills and all the lovely grandparents, uncles, and aunts in their lives who loved them so much and could care for them if Mom went to heaven. I also reminded them that the earth is just a stopping ground, and that we will all, God willing, get to spend eternity together in heaven.

It was such a good reminder for me, realizing that their sweet minds sometimes processed things I had no way of knowing. This experience highlighted the value of counsellors, who so often know the right questions to ask. It's important to create a safe space for children to express their concerns and fears, to help them navigate their journey with greater comfort.

STUDY GUIDE QUESTIONS

1. What are the four C's of grief for children?

2. The author describes her children's fear that she would die too. What are some fears that you have?

3. How do you lean in to Jesus when these fears take over?

Four

UNDERSTANDING WELLNESS

AS I SAT amidst the ashes of my life, bewildered and searching for meaning after the loss of my husband, I realized that wellness was going to play a crucial role in my healing process. With God's grace, Sandra 2.0 decided that she wanted to live abundantly.

The concept of wellness is often associated with physical health, but it encompasses so much more than that. Wellness is a state of mental, physical, social, spiritual, and emotional well-being that allows us to function at our best. Indeed, it allows us to thrive!

The Importance of Wellness

As I began to focus on wellness strategies, I noticed a significant improvement in my quality of life. By embracing wellness strategies, I found that my emotional, mental, and physical health improved tremendously. I also experienced a deeper connection with Jesus and found solace in my faith during my darkest moments.

For example, when I started to work on deep breathing exercises and limited my screen time, I was able to sleep better. When I slept better, I was able to wake up earlier to sit in stillness and try to hear God's voice or feel His presence.

Remember, wellness is an ongoing process that allows us to function optimally both personally and with those in our communities. May you find hope, healing, and strength through Jesus Christ as you embark on your own journey towards wellness.

The Pillars of Wellness

In this chapter, I will discuss four major pillars of wellness: mindset, sleep, activity, and relationships. There are others mentioned in the literature, but these are the ones I would like to discuss in detail.

Mindset. I realized that my mindset plays a crucial role in my personal growth and well-being. As a woman of faith, I learned to lean on my faith and trust in God's plan for me, which helped me overcome fear and apprehension.

I once heard a really cool fact in a prayer meeting. Did you know that the phrase "Do not be afraid" appears in the Bible 365 times? That's once for every day of the year. What a beautiful reminder!

However, if you are struggling with fear and anxiety, this doesn't mean your faith is lacking. Just as with any other medical condition, supportive treatment and management is available through healthcare.

Another shift in mindset involved focusing on the Holy Spirit and the fruits of the Spirit, which was uplifting for me and allowed me to pursue my future with confidence and optimism. I also reflected on the words of Proverbs 3:5–6: *"Trust in the Lord with all your heart, and lean not on your own understanding; in all your ways acknowledge Him, and He shall direct your paths."*

Leaning not on my own understanding is a work in progress. I try to remind myself every day that His ways are higher than my ways.

Sleep. I used to struggle with getting enough quality sleep, but I came to realize how vital sleep is to my overall well-being. I made it a priority to establish a consistent sleep schedule and create a calming bedtime routine. With better sleep, I found myself more energized, focused, and emotionally stable, allowing me to be my best self for my children and community.

Activity. I made a commitment to stay active and incorporate regular exercise into my daily life. I found activities that I genuinely enjoyed, like hiking in nature, running, and strength training. Staying active not only improved my physical health but helped me feel more connected to God's beautiful artwork all around me, which in turn enhanced my spiritual wellness.

Relationships. As a Christian woman, I learned the importance of fostering strong, healthy relationships with those around me. I focused on deepening my connections with my family, friends, and church community by being more present, empathetic, and compassionate. These strengthened relationships not only improved my emotional well-being but reinforced my sense of belonging and support in my faith community.

If you haven't already done so, and if it feels right, you may consider taking baby steps to reconnect with those around you. Even if you just visit for a few minutes, or have a short phone call, try to connect to as many communities as you can. There may be a coworker, a church friend, or a friend at the gym or in your neighbourhood whom you find uplifting. Try to plug in and create that community. That relationship may be a bit different after your experience of grief, but give yourself permission to surround yourself with the people you feel most comfortable with.

I found socializing and sense of community tricky to navigate initially. Suddenly, my life was completely different, and I was completely different. I was exhausted and just wanted to be alone. My first hurdle was wondering if I was able to muster the energy to get out, what would I contribute to the conversation? I don't want to lie and say I am doing well but I didn't want to get into how wrecked I was either. I didn't have the capacity to make my usual lighthearted and cheesy jokes, but I didn't want to sit there with a long face either and dampen the party. Nor did I want my trauma to be the elephant in the room.

What I dreaded most was the looks and whispers people adopted when they first saw me. They would say, pointedly, "How *are* you?" I don't know why this bothered me so much. Maybe I just wanted to be spoken to normally, not like I was a sheet of broken glass. However, we all grieve differently and are sensitive to different things at different times.

I started very slowly connecting with those closest to me, whether that meant returning a phone call or lingering with a visitor at the front door for a few minutes. I found that coming right out and sharing my thoughts or fears alleviated the pressure off our socialization. I eventually became comfortable setting boundaries and expectations ahead of time.

For example, I might have said, "Sure, let's meet at the coffee shop, but I can only stay a very short time and I really don't want to talk about my grief. Could you please not ask about it? I'm also not feeling super chatty. Could we just sit together?"

Communication is essential—and it becomes more important than ever when you're feeling vulnerable. I practiced being honest. Sometimes I would say things like "I would love to see you, but I'm worried it's going to be depressing for you to just sit across from me while I stare into space. I'm not the same person I was before. I don't actually know who I am now."

Be kind to yourself as you try and navigate this new you. The old you is still in there and they're amazing. They're going to heal and have emotional maturity and sensitivity after this experience.

Try to create community wherever you go. Making eye contact and learning people's names are great ways to ensure that they feel seen and noticed.

When I embraced overall wellness, these principles not only enhanced my personal growth and healing but allowed me to be a more active, loving, and supportive member of my church community. I hope my story can serve as an encouragement for you to seek your overall well-being—mentally, physically, and spiritually.

Wellness and Faith

As I continued to grow and develop my wellness strategies, I found that my faith played an essential role. Here's how my spiritual journey intertwined with my wellness journey.

Physical wellness and faith. As I stayed committed to my physical exercise and health, I realized that my body is an incredible gift from God. I felt a sense of gratitude for the strength, flexibility, and endurance that allowed me to fully engage in physical exercise. My faith encouraged me to remain consistent in my efforts regardless of how small they are, knowing that I was honouring God by taking care of the body He gave me.

Emotional/psychological wellness and faith. In the painful times when I struggled with crushing pain, I leaned on my faith for support and guidance. Through prayer, meditation, and reading the Bible, I gained a deeper understanding of myself and my emotions and more clearly focused on the bigger picture of experiencing the kingdom of heaven. This spiritual practice allowed me to develop a healthier mindset, promoting emotional resilience and better emotional and mental well-being.

When I focused on God, which wasn't always easy, I was able to see the big picture. Earth is a very short stop on the route to eternity, which is the real goal. Imagine running to Jesus and His big smile and warm hug! Imagine the pure happiness of that moment. There is no sadness and no fear there, just love. Just Jesus.

It's easier not to sweat the small stuff when you look at the big picture.

Every day our brains process several thousand thoughts. "According to the National Science Foundation, eighty percent of our thoughts are negative and ninety-five percent of our thoughts are repetitive. That is a lot of repetitive and negative thoughts!"[7]

As I started to become aware of my thoughts, I challenged them. I sometimes found myself ruminating, *My life is over. Things will never be good again.* So I challenged that, eventually replacing it with a more balanced thought: *Life is difficult right now, but it will get better.*

---

[7] Charlotte Johnson, "Stuck on Negative Thinking," *Care Counseling*. Date of access: June 20, 2023 (https://care-clinics.com/stuck-on-negative-thinking).

> Every day our brains process around several thousand thoughts. "According to the National Science Foundation, eighty percent of our thoughts are negative and ninety-five percent of our thoughts are repetitive. That is a lot of repetitive and negative thoughts!"

Upon meeting more and more people who had been struggling through grief and trauma, I identified a common thread in all humanity: we want to believe and hope that things will get better, but we have difficulty doing so.

This book has been written with the hope that even one person who is struggling will read it and say, "Wow! Maybe things will get better. God has good things planned for me and He will help me. He will carry me."

Social wellness and faith. As I cultivated stronger relationships with those around me by slowly increasing my interactions, I found that my faith community played a vital role in my social wellness. The support, encouragement, and love I received from my Christian brothers and sisters provided a sense of belonging and acceptance for myself and my children.

As I prayed and spent time with others aligned in my faith, our shared experiences helped us grow together, spiritually and socially. I am especially fond of grabbing a coffee, going for a walk in nature, and praying together. These activities fill me up on so many levels.

Spiritual wellness and faith. My faith journey has been the cornerstone of my spiritual wellness. I dedicated time to nurturing my relationship with God through prayer, attending liturgy, and worship.

This continues to be a work in progress. I still feel betrayed, angry, and abandoned by God at times. But I've decided that I don't want to do life without Him, so I have kept showing up. This connection to God, knowing that no matter how much of a hot mess I feel like, no matter how much I feel like I've failed my kids, prompts me to meditate on these words from Jeremiah 31:3: *"The Lord has appeared of old to me, saying: 'Yes, I have loved you with an everlasting love; therefore with lovingkindness I have drawn you.'"*

This provided me with a sense of purpose and gave me direction, allowing me to live according to my values and maintain a deep love for my Saviour.

Bible Reading

As I read the Bible, I realized how many inspiring role models are found in it. I felt like God had messed up my plans and pondered this as I read about Joseph (sold by his brothers, wrongfully jailed), Ruth (widowed and followed Naomi to her land), and the Virgin Mary (pregnant at a young age, having to watch her Son die). They were people just like me, but they chose to lean into God and continue to trust Him even when they couldn't understand. Saint Mary really inspired me when she said, *"Let it be to me according to your word"* (Luke 1:38).

I read from the prayers and excerpts I had saved on my phone. These are the ones I found particularly hopeful. I read them over and over until I started to believe them.

It has been said that MRI evidence suggests that certain neural pathways are increased when people practice self-affirmation tasks such as repeating positive affirmations daily.[8] I practiced this by reading encouraging verses such as Jeremiah 29:11 and repeating it to myself, *"'For I know the plans I have for you,' declares the Lord, 'plans to prosper you and not to harm you, plans to give you hope and a future'"* (NIV).

---

[8] Christopher N. Cascio, Matthew Brook O'Donnell, Francis J. Tinney, Matthew D. Lieberman, Shelley E. Taylor, Victor J. Strecher, and Emily B. Falk, "Self-Affirmation Activates Brain Systems Associated with Self-Related Processing and Reward and Is Reinforced by Future Orientation." *National Library of Medicine 11(4)*, April 2016, 621–629.

Hymns and Spiritual Songs

I've always been fascinated with music. I love music in almost all genres and all languages. If you've ever heard one of my playlists, you might have laughed at how much of a mishmash it is of all the things I love. You'd hear an Arabic song, followed by Soca music or a worship song or a Coptic hymn. Or perhaps a Greek love song, Spanish party song, or some alternative or punk music. The list could go on.

I have always found a deep connection to music. Listening to music has so many benefits:

1. Music distracts us from fatigue or sadness.
2. Music stimulates the part of the brain that controls movement. This is why a workout can feel a lot more effective and enjoyable when you're listening to heart-pumping tunes.
3. Music improves the mood and increases levels of dopamine and oxytocin in the brain.
4. Music works on the limbic part of the brain which stimulates learning.

Music can also be used to learn new skills, as a form of therapy to heal, and to enhance one's athletic performance. If you grew up in the 90s, you may remember that a way to express your love for someone was to make them a mixtape; you chose songs you loved, wanting to share that great vibe. Although I love most things about the 90s, I'm glad that we've moved on from cassette tapes. It was so hard to rewind to just the right spot for your favourite song!

At my late husband's funeral, his cousin asked me if she could make a CD and distribute it to the guests alongside the prayer card we had prepared. I thought that was such a beautiful sentiment. When I listened to this CD for the first time, it felt like I had tapped into a whole new world. I had never heard worship music before, but suddenly I was listening to Danny Gokey sing a beautiful song about pain and loss and holding on to one's faith. I couldn't believe it!

FOUR: UNDERSTANDING WELLNESS

There is something incredible about listening to music and finding the words your heart longs to scream but couldn't articulate. I am so grateful that I was introduced to worship music at that time, it has played a valuable role in my spiritual life and healing journey.

I played this song over and over. I sprinted to it on the treadmill. I sang along to it in the car. I cried to it in the closet while my children slept. I buried my head in an old dress shirt that still held the lingering smell of my husband's cologne.

The music also lessened my feelings of loneliness. The reason I felt lonely wasn't that I didn't have a beautiful family and friends around me. I did. But you can be in a room full of people and still feel lonely. Have you ever experienced this? It feels awful.

Mother Teresa, who had been all over the world, once said that loneliness was one of the worst diseases she had ever seen.

There were two other songs that spoke to my very core, resonating with exactly the way I felt. I had all these turbulent thoughts and emotions but couldn't sort them out, but these songs were so freeing. I felt that the artists who sang them could relate. I cried to these songs and prayed their lyrics while tilting my tear-soaked face heavenward to God, really hoping that He was listening.

One song was "He Knows," by Jeremy Camp, which spoke to the depth of my heartbreak. The other, which really hit home, was "Just Be Held," by Casting Crowns.

Now, I'm always a person who gets things done. Among my friends and family, I love to have an organized plan and be as helpful as possible. I have become a resource centre for patients, clients, and others in my life. If you're looking for a Sunday school lesson, workout plan, or connection, I'm your girl. I love it that way.

I've always wanted to be a helper. In fact, my name, Sandra, means "helper of mankind." I don't know how helpful I was when I was young and dishes needed to be done, or when my room needed to be cleaned, but I do my best now.

In any case, it was very difficult for me to accept help from others—or, for that matter, to accept my own weakness. Silly, I know.

But that Casting Crowns song, in its opening lines, captivated me. The lyrics were all about holding it together, about life throwing you curveballs that hit you out of nowhere.

These songs were so powerful.

I invite you to listen to these songs or any other hymns or songs of praise that resonate with you. Allow them to release the words that are locked in your throat. For me, this music has been so cathartic.

Arabic isn't my first language, but I speak it relatively well.[9] There is one Arabic hymn I especially loved called "El bahr el hayeg." In it, the artist sings loudly about how she yelled while she was drowning and Jesus came and saved her. Each time I heard this hymn, a neat visual came to me. I pictured myself with the water coming up to my ears, barely treading water, and my limbs on fire. I pictured Jesus smiling down and reaching out to me with so much love and pulling me out.

I used that imagery often, whenever despair threatened to take over.

After any loss, we must journey to find our new identity. I invite you to embrace your new identity in Christ while honouring the past.

My faith has been a constant source of strength, inspiration, and guidance as I continue to strive to be the best version of myself. I hope my story can encourage others as they embark on their own wellness journeys, reminding them that they are never alone in their pursuit of a healthier, more abundant life.

---

[9] Some may disagree!

FOUR: UNDERSTANDING WELLNESS

STUDY GUIDE QUESTIONS

1. Which four pillars of wellness does the author describe?

2. Explain why each of these pillars is important to one's overall well-being.

3. Choose one aspect of wellness and describe how it works alongside your faith.

4. Do you have any hymns or worship songs that comfort you? Some of my favourite are "Even If" (Mercy Me), "Do It Again" (Elevation Worship), "You Say" (Lauren Daigle), "I Am Not Alone" (Kari Jobi), "He Knows" (Jeremy Camp), and "Just Be Held" (Casting Crowns).

Five

STRESS AND WELLNESS

I'VE NOTICED THAT if I don't keep stress in check, it can sometimes have a negative impact on my mental health, such as causing fear to overwhelm me.

We seem to chase a constant state of busyness, or at least I do. I often find that I fill my plate until it's overflowing with no margin or breathing room. Eventually this leads to burnout. With so many commitments and seemingly never enough time, it's likely common for many to feel stressed and overwhelmed.

I've experienced this myself, feeling as if I were constantly being pulled in multiple directions and struggling to stay present. The first physical symptom I notice, or "tell," is that my hair starts to fall out or I develop heartburn.

Another cause of stress can be seeking personal validation and worth in our accomplishments. One of my Christian friends often reminds me, "You are worthy, you are chosen, and you are fearfully and wonderfully made." My identity is in Christ, not in my accomplishments or completed daily tasks.

The Consequences of Stress

Unmanaged stress can harm us physically, emotionally, and mentally. Chronic stress can affect your sleep, immunity, productivity, relationship quality, heart health, and mood. Stress may also affect your overall health if you use unhealthy behaviours to cope. When these behaviours become habits, they can often be identified as stress-induced habits.

When stress takes over, it can be tempting to engage in unhealthy habits as a form of escape—in other words, they become coping mechanisms. During the pandemic, I found that patients started drinking alcohol earlier and earlier, even coining phrases like "It's wine o'clock." Streaming binges and fast food also became commonplace indulgences as people wanted to just numb themselves.

However, the key to counteracting stress is staying present and nurturing your well-being through self-care. I've learned to prioritize connections with the people who matter most to me. Spending quality time with family and friends has been invaluable for my emotional health.

Taking this a step further, I find that the effect is synergistic when I can combine a self-care activity with a loved one. For example, getting together for prayer, great meals, or workouts is particularly enjoyable for me.

Recognizing Stress

Recognizing the signs of stress in your body is essential to managing it. Identify your personal tells and be on the lookout for them. Tells are the signs and symptoms in our bodies that signal we are experiencing stress. Recognizing them is crucial for effective stress management.

These signs and symptoms will vary from person to person. Physical symptoms might include heartburn, headaches, difficulty sleeping, and hair loss. Some people will recognize emotional and behavioural symptoms where they feel more anxious, pick at their skin or bite their nails, and have difficulty concentrating or making decisions.

Managing Stress

I've come to understand that managing stress is about more than just surrounding myself with loved ones. It's important to strike a balance

FIVE: STRESS AND WELLNESS

between my personal life, work, and other commitments. For me, this has meant making a conscious effort to create a carefree, happy, and loving space at home. I've also set aside a special corner in my room for prayer and quiet time.

On those days when I've felt like I was hanging on by a thread, I've learned to ask for help or delegate tasks. This is challenging for me, but I continue to learn how essential it is. It's allowed me to create space for rest and relaxation, which is indispensable for my mental health.

Dealing with stress is inevitable. We will dive into relaxation and self-care strategies in a later chapter.

STUDY GUIDE QUESTIONS

1. Do you either create margin for yourself or leave free time in your schedule?

2. What is one thing you can do this upcoming week to create space in your schedule?

3. What are your physical tells that reveal when you're stressed? For example, it could be headaches, heartburn, hair loss, etc.

4. What spiritual practice helps you the most when you are feeling overwhelmed?

RELATIONSHIPS AND WELLNESS

THROUGHOUT MY HEALING journey, I've come to recognize the crucial role that interpersonal connections play in maintaining wellness. I've learned the importance of building trust, empathy, and understanding, and how these factors contribute to a wonderful social support system.

The pandemic took a huge toll on the physical and mental health of many people. It was devastating for our churches, schools, and workplaces to close and be cut off from our usual activities and interactions.

Research suggests that individuals with strong and healthy relationships experience many benefits, including lower rates of anxiety and depression, increased empathy, and higher self-esteem. These positive effects have a direct impact on one's personal health and overall well-being.[10]

As I've grown older, I've found it essential to continue nurturing my relationships to maintain good mental and physical health. It's easy for me to become very busy and get back into that rinse-and-repeat pattern which doesn't leave much room for social interaction.

I try not to let this happen, though. I've noticed that when daily tasks become overwhelming or my social connections weaken, it affects my overall well-being.

---

[10] "Strong Relationships, Strong Health," *Better Health*. February 24, 2022 (https://www.betterhealth.vic.gov.au/health/healthyliving/Strong-relationships-strong-health).

I've made a conscious effort to engage in regular social and spiritual activities as well as maintain close relationships with friends and family. This has helped me manage stress, reduce the risk of chronic illnesses, and maintain a positive outlook on my life.

Here are some tips for how to cultivate healthy relationships.

- Engage in some self-reflection on your own values, needs, and boundaries.
- Communicate openly and honestly, listen actively, and show genuine interest in what others have to say.
- Build trust by being reliable and keeping your promises.
- Respect and encourage one another.
- Spend quality time and share activities to deepen your relationships.
- Discover each other's love languages.

If you aren't already familiar with the five love languages, I invite you to learn more about this important subject. Gary Chapman's book, *The Five Love Languages*,[11] is a game-changer, packed full of valuable information to help us better understand how we express and receive love.

The five love languages are: words of affirmation, acts of service, receiving gifts, quality time, and physical touch.

The benefits of understanding your own love language, and that of your loved ones, allow you to communicate love more effectively and will help you cultivate wellness in your relationships.

---

[11] Gary Chapman, *The Five Love Languages* (Chicago, IL: Moody Publishing, 2014).

SIX: RELATIONSHIPS AND WELLNESS

STUDY GUIDE QUESTIONS

1. How have strong connections positively impacted your wellness? Share a specific example.

2. Think of at least two people who you feel are a blessing in your life. Consider writing them a thank-you note or text and say a prayer for them.

MEDITATION AND MINDFULNESS

WHAT IS MINDFULNESS? Let me start by acknowledging that meditation has been a game-changer in my wellness journey.

Meditating is what happens when you focus your mind on a particular activity, thought, or object. Meditation is a big buzzword in the healthcare literature, and for good reason. Practicing meditation daily may produce calmness and clarity.

Mindful meditation is what happens when we're thoughtful and present in everything we do.

Biblical Meditation

Personally, I've fallen in love with biblical meditation. It's not something I can do on my own, but I try to draw near to God and ask Him to help me. I ask Him to allow His thoughts and ways to be known to me so I can see my circumstances from a holy perspective.

I don't think I'll ever know why my family endured our loss—not on this side of heaven, in any case. I do, however, choose to believe that God will work all these circumstances for our good.

When I choose to spend as little as five minutes on biblical meditation, I choose to shift my focus to the God who is the Word and off myself and my fears. I ask Him to look into my heart and remove anything that isn't pleasing to Him, helping to transform my thoughts and mind to align with His plan for me.[12]

---

[12] There's an app called "Bible" that contains plans that allow you to go through guided biblical meditations. I highly recommend it.

As someone whose natural speed of life is very fast, it takes constant reminders for me to slow down and focus my thoughts entirely on the task at hand, whether it's loading the dishwasher or running on the treadmill. The idea is to focus your mind on the present.

The Benefits of Mindfulness

Mindfulness meditation can help with mental health disorders. The benefits are mainly derived from the fact that it allows people to focus on their experiences and feelings in the moment and practice having a positive attitude about what's happening. This is how meditation helps restore the mind and body connection balance.

One of my colleagues in healthcare offers very popular mindfulness-based stress reduction (MBSR) sessions. Research shows that MBSR is effective at reducing stress as well as improving symptoms of burnout.[13]

The following are the steps that work for me when it comes to managing stress:

- Recognize your feelings and acknowledge them.
- Remind yourself that the stress is temporary and that God has a plan for you.
- Practice having a positive attitude about what's happening around you through prayer and gratitude.

Gratitude

When it comes to mindfulness, gratitude plays an important role. Gratitude is about being mindful of and appreciating the various aspects of our lives.

Several studies have shown that people who practice gratitude are less likely to feel stress. They report having an improved quality of life.[14]

---

[13] "MBSR: Mindfulness-Based Stress Reduction," *Brown University School of Public Health*. Date of access: July 25, 2019 (https://www.apa.org/topics/mindfulness/meditation).

[14] "Practicing Gratitude," *News in Health*. Date of access: June 20, 2023 (https://newsinhealth.nih.gov/2019/03/practicing-gratitude).

SEVEN: MEDITATION AND MINDFULNESS

You can start a gratitude journal or visualize at least three things you are grateful for daily. Practicing gratitude can rewire your brain positively.

Practicing mindfulness can be challenging but ultimately rewarding as it helps you to become more patient and at peace with yourself.

> Rejoice always, pray without ceasing, in everything give thanks; for this is the will of God in Christ Jesus for you. (1 Thessalonians 5:16–18)

I always loved that verse. It's so simple: rejoice, pray, and be thankful in all circumstances.

I had an exceptionally difficult time rejoicing and being thankful during my loss. I was barely able to pray. I kept showing up, though. I was angry and beaten, but I tried every day to pray or read the Bible.

Some days were harder than the others. I asked God to help me, and the Holy Spirit to work in me, because on my own I wasn't even close to attaining joy or gratitude. I wanted to reach the point where I could mindfully reflect on all the things I was grateful for, the good and the bad. This has continued to be a work in progress.

Mindfulness is a powerful type of meditation that focuses on being present and living in the moment instead of dwelling on past events or worrying about the future.

For me, as I've mentioned, it can be very challenging to slow down and be still. God often calls us to be still and sit with Him. It's easier for me to complete a challenging forty-five-minute athletic class than to lay still for two to three minutes during the cooldown. Sometimes that which is most difficult is the thing we need most. It's certainly true in my case. When I do manage to slow down, I am less snappy and more at peace.

When practicing mindfulness without self-judgment, you become aware of what you're seeing, hearing, and feeling. Start by finding time to clear your mind. Then take slow deep breaths while grounding yourself in the present moment, which can reduce stress and lead to clearer thinking.

I have a lot of room to grow in this regard, but I try to approach it in bite-sized strides. When I'm eating, for example—pun intended!

You can practice mindfulness while you're taking a walk, loading the dishwasher, or handling any daily activity. You just tune in to the experience. In the process, you may be surprised at how enjoyable it is to get out of your head for a little while.

I once read a book filled with daily meditations written for busy moms so they could find the time to meet with Jesus daily. One of those writers reiterated what my colleagues in mental health frequently talk about, which is the power of thinking "I *have* to…" versus "I *get* to…" I often find myself thinking, "Ahh, I have to pack lunches, do laundry, and pay the bills…" However, I can shift the narrative to something more positive: "I get to do laundry, which I am grateful for because it means I have the ability to purchase clothing for all seasons. I'm blessed to have clean clothing to wear and a family which will be kept warm and happy!" This has filled my life with much more joy and much less grumbling.

As Philippians 2:14 gently reminds us, *"Do all things without complaining and disputing…"* Coating our thoughts with gratitude is a great start.

Emotional Stress

The connection between physical and mental health is significant when it comes to emotional stress, which often leads to physical pain, illness, and disease. Emotional stress has been known to be related to many chronic illnesses, such as high blood pressure and heart disease.[15]

Studies have shown that naturally happy and optimistic people tend to be healthier than their pessimistic counterparts. Some studies

---

[15] "Stress," *Centre for Addiction and Mental Health.* Date of access: June 20, 2023 (https://www.camh.ca/en/health-info/mental-illness-and-addiction-index/stress).

even show that religious people live longer on average than secular people, partly due to the overall positive attitude that being religious gives them.[16] The mind-body connection works both ways: how you feel can affect your body's health, but how your body is can also affect how you feel mentally.

It's important to note that the mind-body connection isn't limited to physical health. Emotional stress can have a negative effect on one's mental health.

For many people, meditation is an effective way to cope with negative emotions and thoughts.

A Look Inside the Mind-Body Connection

The mind-body connection plays a crucial role in both physical and mental well-being. Research suggests that positive emotions and positive thoughts improve your overall health. On the other hand, stress, anxiety, and negative emotions can cause inflammatory responses, which may contribute to heart disease.[17]

It's no surprise that separating your mental health from your physical state can be very difficult. When you're in a good mental space, it often reflects positively on your physical state. However, when you're struggling mentally, it can be tough to maintain physical wellness. We often feel down about ourselves when we aren't in a good situation. As it turns out, this doesn't have to be the case. It's essential to remember that we can still make a difference.

Many diseases and health issues stem from stress and negative emotions. Some of these diseases may appear to come out of nowhere, but they are often caused by long-term emotional issues

---

[16] "Religion's Relationship to Happiness, Civic Engagement, and Health Around the World," *Pew Research Center*. January 31, 2019 (https://www.pewresearch.org/religion/2019/01/31/religions-relationship-to-happiness-civic-engagement-and-health-around-the-world).

[17] Karen Feldscher, "Take It to Heart: Positive Emotions May Be Good for Health," *Harvard School of Public Health*. August 15, 2011 (https://www.hsph.harvard.edu/news/features/positive-emotions-health-kubzansky-html).

that have been festering inside us for years. If you think about it, our minds and bodies work in tandem. By nurturing this connection, we can overcome challenges and maintain a balanced life.

It's a common misconception that our mental health is separate from our physical health, but the truth is that they are deeply interconnected.

To improve our overall well-being, there are certain practices we can incorporate into our daily lives to enhance both our mental and physical health.

Mindfulness is a technique many people use to relax and recharge, but mindfulness is also an effective tool to improve one's mental health.

One of the reasons that mindfulness is effective for improving mental health is because it allows us to be present. Being present means that we're so absorbed in whatever we're doing that we don't notice anything else around us.

Think about how you feel when you're at work or school, completely focused and free from interruptions or distractions. That's what it's like to be fully present.

One simple and accessible approach to mindfulness involves focusing on your breathing. It's one of the easiest ways to be mindful in your daily activities, and to have a positive approach to life in general.

Square breathing is very popular and was taught to my children at their school. It's also known as the "four-by-four technique" or "box breathing." Focus on inhaling for four counts while expanding the diaphragm. Then exhale for four counts while releasing the air. If your thoughts wander, gently guide them back and tether your mind to your breathing.

Mindfulness Benefits All Aspects of Health

To truly embrace mindfulness, it's important to practice it consistently, allowing the benefits to spill over into other aspects of your life. Once

SEVEN: MEDITATION AND MINDFULNESS

you've gotten in the habit of practicing this, you can use the same practice in other ways, such as to improve your mental health.

When we focus on our breathing during meditation—and when we're otherwise focused on other things, like concentrating on work or trying out a new recipe for dinner—we're better able to be present with whatever is going on around us and within ourselves.

Other strategies for improving mental health include:

- Exercising for at least thirty minutes a day.
- Eating healthy food in moderation.
- Spending quality time with your friends and family on a regular basis, as well as with God.
- Taking time out of your day to do things you love and make you happy.

In fact, there are many things you can do regularly to improve your mental health and well-being. That's why it's important to make an effort to do these things consistently, whether once a week or several times a day.

Remember that everyone's path to mental health will be different. Also, everyone's version of mental health is different. You might be able to do things in a way that works for you, but another person may not do things in the same way. It's essential to find what works for you and your lifestyle.

One other important realization about mindful meditation is that it can be done anywhere at any time. For example, you could stop to take a deep breath and relax your mind and body as much as possible throughout the day. Remember that the mind-body connection isn't a one-way street. We aren't just physical beings with minds; we're also conscious, thinking beings.

STUDY GUIDE QUESTIONS

1. How does Bible meditation help with wellness?

2. Philippians 2:14 talks about grumbling. What is something you often grumble about? Can you change your mentality from *having* to do it to instead *getting* to do it?

3. What are three strategies for improving your mental health? Which of these strategies would you like to incorporate into your weekly schedule?

4. Take a moment to read a Bible verse of your choice and meditate on it for two to three minutes in silence. For example, consider Psalm 25:5: *"Guide me in your truth and teach me, for you are God my Savior, and my hope is in you all day long"* (NIV).

Eight

EXERCISE

I COULD TALK all day and all night about how essential exercise will be in your journey. I love exercise! If all the benefits of exercise could be bottled into a tablet, it would be the most expensive and magical pill.

Exercise can lower blood sugar and reduce the occurrence of heart attacks, certain cancers, heart disease, osteoporosis, anxiety, and depression while improving muscle tone, endorphins, and mood.[18]

How Exercise Impacted My Healing

My first experience with the healing effects of exercise came on the day of my late husband's funeral. As the funeral drew to a close, I was left with a surge of restless energy and an impending sense of hysteria. Knowing that I couldn't bear to head home just yet, I found myself at the local gym. I went to the pool to swim laps. Immersing myself in water proved to be incredibly therapeutic. Even looking at the water was comforting.

With each stroke of my arms and kick of my legs, I unleashed an explosion of emotions, directing my anguished questions towards God: "Why, God? *Why?* How are we going to survive?" My body pushed forward while my mind screamed for answers,

---

[18] "Benefits of Physical Activity," *Centers for Disease Control and Prevention*. Date of access: June 16, 2022 (https://www.cdc.gov/physicalactivity/basics/pa-health/index.htm).

creating a cathartic experience that allowed me to breathe just a little bit easier.

Earlier in my life, during my maternity leave for my daughter, I desperately needed to get out of the house and move. I was blessed to find a wonderful mom and baby fitness group that I was able to attend with a great friend. We took our strollers for walks while we lunged. We sat under a tree or in the studio with our babies facing us on a mat or in the baby carrier on our chests. We laughed, we worked up a sweat, we listened to music, and most essential of all we created community. This is where I learned about the huge value of group therapy — and that is what it was, unofficially.

At the end of the class, we sat in a big circle and all shared how we were doing. It wasn't uncommon for a mom to burst into tears because she was overwhelmed with worry or felt like she was doing a bad job. "I constantly live in my rattiest clothing and am so sleep-deprived!" "Sleep training is so stressful!" "The baby is teething, and we are struggling!" Some moms gave practical tips about what had helped them, and others murmured their sympathy and ability to relate. So much comfort can be found by being part of a support group.

Exercising for as little as ten-minute bouts at moderate intensity can reap several health benefits. It could be nothing more complicated than a brisk walk around the block.

I personally find exercise to be essential, not just for my physical health, but for my mental health as well. I was so inspired by the fitness community that I started co-teaching a class with the instructor who had graciously mentored me. I then pursued my fitness instructor certification. I love creating movement and community.

If you've ever attended my classes, you'll know I am a big believer in community. I'll encourage you to introduce yourself to others and encourage one another. Also, I often wear shirts that really entertain me, and hopefully others as well. My current favourite has a picture of a needle and thread and says "Can you sew? ...Cuz I'm RIPPED!" Baddum-ching!

Okay, I'll see myself out.

Don't forget what Proverbs 17:22 tells us: *"A merry heart does good, like medicine..."* I try to laugh whenever I can.

The mood benefits and physical outlet were incredibly helpful to me during my grief. They continue to support my well-being. There are so many beautiful options for getting good exercise!

When I first started incorporating physical activity into my daily routine, I noticed a significant improvement in my mood. Exercise helps lower the stress hormones released by the adrenal gland, which are responsible for feelings of fear, worry, and anxiety. As I committed to exercising regularly, my energy levels increased and I felt more motivated and less fatigued. Plus, adding worship music helped to reduce my worries even further.

As time went by, I realized that exercise had become a crucial part of my mental health recovery. My body was growing physically stronger through regular workouts, causing my mental strength and resilience to improve as well. The crushing and suffocating pain in my chest began to ease and I felt more in control of my emotions.

I noticed an incredible boost in my self-esteem. I had been feeling beat down as opposed to the capable woman I had once viewed myself to be. Exercise helped me regain that confidence in myself.

Today, I continue to prioritize exercise as an essential component of my wellness journey. By staying committed to movement, I've been able to maintain a healthier state of mind and overall well-being. The psychological benefits of exercise have been so helpful, and I'm grateful for the improvement this has produced in my quality of life.

Before you do anything more vigorous than walking, though, it's a good idea to get the approval of your family doctor. This is especially important if you have any medical conditions, are injured or pregnant, or have any other concerns.

Benefits of Exercise

One of the most significant advantages of regular exercise is its ability to boost cardiovascular health. Cardiovascular disease is the number one leading cause of death in women.[19] By engaging in aerobic activities, such as swimming, cycling, dancing, or running, you can strengthen your heart and lungs, reduce your risk of heart disease, and improve blood circulation. This in turn can help lower your blood pressure.

Exercise can also improve sleep. When my grief was fresh, my sleep suffered terribly. Regular physical activity can help improve the overall quality of your sleep, which is essential to function optimally and boost your overall well-being.

Exercise has also been shown to have a positive impact on your immune system. Regular exercise can help your body fight off infections and reduce inflammation, which is essential for maintaining overall health and wellness.

Exercise has many mental health benefits, including reducing symptoms of depression and anxiety, relieving stress, and improving self-esteem.[20] To make the most of these benefits, consider incorporating mindfulness practices into your routine. This can help you connect with your body and mind, fostering a sense of well-being.

Another unexpected benefit I discovered was the anti-aging effects. Research shows that people who exercise regularly have biological markers almost a decade younger than those who don't exercise.[21]

Remember that your wellness journey is unique to you. Be patient with yourself and listen to your body as you progress. I have pushed through injuries by not listening to my body and come to regret it.

---

[19] "Women and Heart Disease," *Centers for Disease Control and Prevention*. May 15, 2023 (https://www.cdc.gov/heartdisease/women.htm).

[20] Ashish Sharma, Vishal Madaan, and Frederick D. Petty, "Exercise for Mental Health." *The Primary Care Companion to the Journal of Clinical Psychiatry 8(2)*, 2006, 106.

[21] Amanda Macmillan, "Exercise Makes You Younger at the Cellular Level," *Time*. May 15, 2017 (https://time.com/4776345/exercise-aging-telomeres).

You'll get the most out of your fitness routine if you listen to your body and remember the importance of recovery, hydration, and nutrition.

Moving and caring for our bodies, which have been gifted to us by God, is a great way to honour Him.

Different Types of Exercise

There are many different types of exercises, each offering unique benefits. Choosing the right activities will depend on factors such as your goals, fitness level, and personal interests.

Once you are cleared for exercise by your primary care provider, there are so many great options to choose from. A lot of research supports the mental health benefits of being in nature. Whether you can safely walk outside or swim laps, being in fresh air or in the water can boost your mental well-being. I'm a big fan of high-intensity interval training (HIIT), sprint interval training (SIT) and functional strength training. There's also Pilates, boxing, and dance. To help you move, don't forget about the music. Zumba gives me a lot of joy too!

Walking. Walking can be very beneficial in bouts of as little as ten minutes. When possible, walking outside is particularly beneficial due to the mental health boost of being in nature. Chair exercises offer an alternative option for people with limited mobility or injuries. There are a variety of "sit and be fit" exercises which can add variety to seated exercises.

Aerobics or cardio. Essential for heart health and overall fitness, aerobic activities include swimming, cycling, running, dancing, and many sports that elevate your heartrate. For people with osteoporosis, you will want to make sure you're getting in some weight-bearing exercises, meaning that you essentially carry your body weight to strengthen the bones. For example, while swimming and cycling are great exercises they are not considered weight bearing exercises.[22]

---

[22] To learn more about exercising with osteoporosis, check out the Osteoporosis Canada website (https://osteoporosis.ca) or https://www.nhs.uk/conditions/osteoporosis/prevention/ . These are excellent resources.

I once saw two friends in a shopping mall who enjoyed fun shirts as much as I do. They wore matching tops that said "Shopping is my cardio." I thought that was cute.

Strength training. Health Canada recommends at least engaging in two strength sessions per week to develop lean muscle strength and mass. This doesn't mean you need to get to a gym and use a heavy barbell, however, even though heavy squats and deadlifts are among my favourites. You can use body weight, bands, dumbbells, and kettlebells as well as train in the comfort of your own home.

Balance, coordination, and flexibility. Exercises like stretching, tai chi, and Pilates are particularly important. These activities enhance balance and flexibility, helping to prevent injury while improving your lifts and movements by allowing for a greater range of motion.

Exploring different exercise types allows you to address various aspects of your physical health while keeping you entertained and engaged. Finding activities that you enjoy is also key to consistency, ultimately leading to long-term health benefits.

With a busy schedule and two very young children, I needed to find creative ways to stay active, even if it meant squeezing in short workouts whenever I could. I would lunge-walk around the playground while the children played, or do counter push-ups and deep squats in the kitchen while cooking. Do whatever works for you! If you look for opportunities, you will find them.

Incorporating Exercise into Daily Life

Incorporating exercise into your daily life is a great way to improve your overall wellness. If you want to start exercising but aren't sure how to start, it's helpful to go slowly at the beginning and gradually increase the intensity and duration of your workouts. It's also helpful to choose activities that you enjoy and can easily integrate into your regular routine. This will help you stay motivated and committed to your program and crush those goals.

Combining movement and community will have a wonderful and synergistic effect. Consider having a friend join you, or joining a class and getting connected to the people there.

My best advice is to move as often as you can. If you can just put on some music at home and a workout video, try that.[23] If you have a sedentary job, get up frequently. Consider standing every hour and doing some gentle stretches. Don't forget to stay hydrated.

You may consider starting with ten minutes of moderate-intensity movement three times per week, outdoors if possible. This will lower your stress hormones and increase your feel-good hormones.

Inviting a friend to exercise with you can also be encouraging. Another strategy is to combine activities, if you're short on time. I like to park far away from my destination. For example, you could park ten minutes down the street from a coffee shop, then sit there with a friend and enjoy a decaf latte with almond milk. My personal favourite.

It can take some practice to be mindful while moving, but the rewards are great.

At first I had difficulty resisting the urge to scroll or type on my phone, but once I focused on soaking in my surroundings and enjoying real-world experiences, I found them to be soothing. For just a few minutes at a time, I could be free from worry about the future or sadness about the past; I could just exist in the present.

Exercise and increased movement can have profound benefits for your overall wellness. I encourage you to also associate exercise with healthy thoughts.

For example, there is one trend in the fitness industry that I personally do not adopt: the mentality that says "Let's burn off that Thanksgiving stuffing" or "Let's burn off that cake." This implies that we need to punish ourselves for enjoying food, that an indulgence must be earned. These thoughts may not help you develop a healthy mental relationship with food.

---

[23] My personal suggestion is to use FitON.

I promote a balanced approach to eating which may include consuming nutritious foods the majority of the time. This produces many wonderful benefits while also leaving room for less nutritious foods we nonetheless enjoy.

However, I don't agree with feeling shame or guilt for taking the occasional indulgence. Enjoy your food and don't feel like you need to punish yourself. Exercise is not punishment for what you've eaten; it's a celebration of what your body can do.

> Exercise is not punishment for what you've eaten; it's a celebration of what your body can do.

I participate in all types of exercise from Pilates to boxing to swimming. I also love many different styles and intensities. Strength training activities, like weightlifting, have been especially helpful for improving my overall physical health. Even with limitations on my time, I found that strength training was accessible and beneficial.

Tips for Beginners

Starting a fitness journey can be intimidating, especially when you have little time and don't know where to start. Here are some tips that you may find useful.

Start small and build up. Start exercising for short periods of time and gradually increase the duration and/or frequency. By starting with just ten minutes a day and slowly increasing it, you can build a sustainable exercise routine without feeling overwhelmed.

Track your progress. Many fitness apps can help you track your workouts and nutrition. You can also opt for journaling or notetaking. This can help you stay focused and motivated. When you're tracking your progress, you can spot trends and follow your progress over time, helping you maintain accountability.

Change it up. To prevent boredom and keep yourself engaged in both mind and body, regularly switch up your workout routine. I like to stay on a progressive course for approximately six weeks. However, within that timeframe I'll change my music as well as some of the exercises and equipment I use. This helps me maintain my excitement and keeps me feeling eager to continue.

Find a workout buddy. Exercising with a friend, family member, or coworker provides an extra layer of accountability and encouragement. It's much harder to let someone else down. I also feel that having a workout partner makes the entire process more enjoyable. You can cheer each other on and get some social benefit. Group fitness classes at your community centre or local gym can also be a great way to make new friends and keep each other accountable.

Be prepared. Before starting your exercise sessions, consider having everything you'll need prepared ahead of time. I find that packing my gym bag the night before is helpful. That way, I'm not running around in a frenzy trying to find my water bottle or clean clothing before the scheduled workout. That preparation can help me stay focused and committed to the plan.

Focus on fitness goals, not just weight loss. Instead of obsessing over the number on the scale, I always encourage my clients to focus on improving their overall fitness level. If you focus on being able to walk for twenty minutes straight or do ten push-ups in a row instead of your weight, research tells us you are more likely to stay motivated and enjoy the process.

Keep moving throughout the day. I make it a point to incorporate movement into my daily routine, even in small ways, like squatting while brushing my teeth or taking some extra steps around the house. These little actions add up. Our beautiful bodies are made to move. We are more mobile and less injury-prone when we spend more time moving and less time sitting.

Exercise in the morning. Whenever possible, I start my day with a workout. This allows me to kick off the day feeling energized and accomplished, setting a positive tone for the rest of the day. It also allows me to fill up my cup before I pour into others for the rest of the day.

That being said, the best time to exercise is going to be different for everyone based on their schedule. As long as it's not within three hours of your bedtime, which can decrease your quality of sleep, fit in your exercise anytime you can.

Connect with others. You can access greater motivation and encouragement by engaging with other people at the gym. This will help you stay accountable and committed to your routine.

Use motivating music or videos. I've discovered that having a go-to playlist or finding workout videos on YouTube makes my exercise sessions much more enjoyable and often turns a good workout into a great one.

STUDY GUIDE QUESTIONS

1. What are three tips for those who are new to exercising?

2. What is one way you can incorporate exercise into your day? For example, you could take a ten-minute walk during your lunch hour a few days per week, or you could take a class or use an exercise video.

3. How does exercise help you spiritually? What spiritual component can you add to your exercise routine?

Nine

NUTRITION

SOME PEOPLE LIVE to eat, relishing every morsel of their meals. Others view food as a necessity for survival.

I fall in the latter category. My family often jokingly recoils as I grab something cold and bland from the fridge like a few boiled eggs, unsalted, and eat them with no fanfare. Or I might have a sad sandwich with no condiments or accompaniments. Instead of a salad, I might just wash romaine lettuce and munch on a leaf by itself. Food, to me, is fuel and medicine.

Of course, that doesn't mean food can't be enjoyed. I just prefer to expend my efforts elsewhere. But for the sake of my children, I have attempted to make the meals nutritious, tasty, and kid-friendly. Part of healthy eating is enjoying your meal with all your senses.

Thank goodness for all the grandparents and aunties who have helped us! And thank God for the internet and all the recipes I've stumbled across.

My mom came to Canada when she was very young. When she wanted to try an old recipe from back home in Egypt, she'd have to wait a few weeks for her own mother to forward the recipe by mail. I'm so glad that nowadays we can search online for almost anything our hearts desire!

The Importance of Eating Well

When we eat well, we improve our overall well-being, manage our weight more effectively, improve our mental health, increase our energy levels, better maintain healthy skin and hair, boost the immune system, and reduce our risk of developing chronic conditions like heart disease, hypertension, osteoporosis, colon cancer, and type-2 diabetes.

In short, I've discovered the importance of feeding my body with wholesome foods and noticing the impact it has on my body. I now pay more attention to the types of food I consume and make a conscious effort to choose healthier options, prioritizing foods with high nutritional content.

My faith has encouraged me to treat my body as a temple of the Holy Spirit, and proper nutrition is a way for me to honour and care for myself, leading to better overall health in mind, body, and spirit.

Let's talk about the importance of nutrition and mental health. There is a very important gut-brain connection, and food can impact our mental health alongside our immune function, bones, and muscles. Eating primarily whole, unprocessed foods can help with symptoms of anxiety and depression. Foods that affect our brain heath tend to contain many great nutrients, such as omega fatty acids, vitamin B, amino acids, minerals, and vitamin D3.

Strive for Balanced Eating

When we choose foods that reduce inflammation and reduce those that increase inflammation, we help prevent certain diseases and cancers. Some foods that can reduce inflammation are fish, nuts, fruits, veggies, and turmeric. Some foods that may cause inflammation include refined sugars, pre-packaged foods, white bread, and pastries.

I'd like to speak about sugar specifically. Sugar is found in many unexpected foods, even crackers and pasta sauce. It also goes by so many different names, which makes it important to read food labels. The order in which ingredients are listed also matters. I once picked up a so-called healthy granola bar and saw that it contained sugar—in fact, sugar was the first ingredient listed. Since ingredients are listed in descending order of quantity, the first ingredient is the most abundant one. Therefore, this bar was mostly made from sugar, with a few oats and other things added to it.

To help you identify added sugars, here are some common sugar synonyms to watch for: dextrose, fructose, glucose, lactose, maltose, honey, agave, cane juice, date sugar, cane sugar, Florida crystals, blackstrap molasses, corn syrup, and high fructose corn syrup.

Added sugar can cause a spike in blood sugar which leads to increased insulin levels and subsequent fat storage. Refined sugars can also stimulate dopamine, which can trigger sugar cravings. We know that sugar can also cause increased inflammation in the body, so it's important to remain aware of how much sugar we are consuming to protect our overall health.

When I read labels, I look for the following values per serving: less than five grams of sugar, more than five grams of fibre, and more than ten grams of protein. Also remember to watch out for saturated fats, which are the harmful artery-clogging fats. Good fats, or monounsaturated fatty acids (MUFAs), are good for health and satiety. Examples are avocados, nuts, and olives. They are calorie dense, however, so do be mindful of your serving size.

I love almond butter and get the natural kind without added sugars and salt. Left unchecked, I could probably eat that by the spoonful. This is why portion control is important. One serving of nuts is considered approximately a quarter cup, as opposed to just taking several handfuls out of the jar. For an avocado, one serving is one-third of an avocado.

Portion control is important so that we eat a balanced variety of nutrients. There are great handouts that help when it comes to determining appropriate portions. They help you visualize your portion based on common objects.

For example, a serving of protein is about the size of a deck of cards. A serving of carbohydrates is about the size of a hockey puck. A serving of fats is about one tablespoon. Canada's Food Guide uses the plate method, which I have used for many years to educate diabetic patients. This is ideal for maintaining balanced blood sugar and nutrient consumption.

According to the plate method, half the plate should be filled with green leafy vegetables or vegetables with bright colours. Consuming orange and green vegetables is recommended, due to their phytonutrients. A quarter of the plate should be devoted to a lean protein source, such as chicken, fish, tofu, tempeh, or beans. The last quarter should have complex carbohydrates. For carbs, look for those that have a low glycemic index, meaning they won't spike your blood sugar.

Why don't you want to spike your blood sugar? A blood sugar spike can cause mood changes, increased insulin, increased fat storage, and increased cravings for sugary foods. My favourite grains are potatoes (either white or sweet), bulghur, couscous, quinoa, and occasionally brown rice.

No Foods Are Good or Bad

A particular campaign used for many years to educate about healthy eating goes by the name "Go, Slow, and Whoa."[24] What I really like about this program is that it uses language that promotes a healthy relationship with food. No food is considered *bad*. Rather, it'll be called a *once in a while* food, because it has lower nutritional value and we want to ensure that we get enough nutritionally dense foods to fuel and strengthen our bodies.

According to this classification system, a food with excellent nutritional value will be coded green (Go). These foods should be eaten most often and are lowest in fats, added sugars, and calories. This category includes fruits, vegetables, whole grains, nuts, and lean meats.

---

[24] Mary L. Gavin, "Go, Slow, and Whoa! A Kid's Guide to Eating Right," *KidsHealth*. March 2022 (https://kidshealth.org/en/kids/go-slow-whoa.html).

A food that is higher in fats, added sugars, or fats is coded yellow (Slow) and is recommended to be eaten only occasionally. This includes items like juice, salad dressings, and cheese sauces.

A food that is much higher in fat or added sugar is coded red (Whoa). It's recommended that these foods be eaten least often, or only once in a while. These include fruit snacks, fries, muffins, and bacon.

Nutritious Snack Ideas

Enjoying balanced meals with high-quality whole foods can have a great impact on your physical and mental health, well-being, and energy levels. Be mindful of portion sizes and always read the labels.

When consuming snacks, note that a balanced snack generally contains two macronutrients. For example, instead of just having berries, you might consider adding cottage cheese or some nuts as added protein. This will make it a more filling snack.

Here are some of my favourite healthy snack combinations:

- fresh fruit and plain Greek yogurt
- apple slices and nut butter
- peaches with soft tofu
- energy balls (oats, dates, nuts, and chia seeds)
- veggie sticks and hummus
- crackers and cheese
- guacamole and bell peppers
- a boiled egg and sliced tomatoes

Identifying Different Types of Hunger

We often talk about emotional eating, throwing around terms such as "a sad day cookie." But food is meant to fuel us and provide nourishment, not comfort. Every time you eat something today, I invite you to ask yourself whether the type of hunger you're experiencing is related to the mouth, the heart, or the stomach.

- Stomach hunger: a physical necessity for fuelling the body.
- Mouth hunger: a craving related to the senses (salty, sweet crunchy).
- Heart hunger: an emotional trigger or learned behaviour.[25]

Once you have determined the type of hunger you're feeling, you can decide what to do. If it's not stomach hunger, what could you do instead of eating? Remember that drinking water is a core weight loss factor for a reason. We often confuse hunger for thirst. Ensuring proper hydration is a helpful tool in determining whether you're actually hungry.

Awareness is key. Do you actually need to eat or can you satisfy your hunger with some other type of activity, such as going for a brisk walk or practicing some deep breathing after an emotional trigger.

If this is a real challenge for you, a dietitian or mental health professional working in this field could support you.

The Hunger Scale
Have you heard of the hunger scale? This scale allows you to rank your hunger, with one signifying that you're incredibly hungry and ten signifying that you're incredibly full.

While attending a particular seminar, we were asked what number on the scale we often ate to. I assumed the answer would be a nine or ten.

Growing up Egyptian, even my non-Egyptian friends knew to come to our home only when they were hungry. Culturally for us, it was a show of hospitality to feed guests until they couldn't possibly manage another bite. Egyptians show their love through food.

If you visit any Middle Eastern home, most of the time you will be offered food and drink even before you have a chance to sit down. The hosts will offer up a large array of appetizers. It would be considered

---

[25] "Types of Hunger," *Craving Change*. Date of access: June 21, 2023 (https://www.cravingchange.ca/wp-content/uploads/2017/08/Types-of-Hunger.pdf).

impolite for a guest to leave food on their plate, so they would finish it even if they were already full.

I later learned that not all cultures celebrate food in this way. Some would place tiny portions of food on their plates; I was astonished to see how much of the plate I could still see when they had finished "filling" their plate.

I love learning about different cultures, foods, costumes, dances, and traditions. Learning the differences in quantity and type of food from one culture to another amazed me.

At that seminar, I learned that our goal in eating should be to reach approximately six or seven on the hunger scale—not nine or ten. The goal of eating should be to enjoy the food and eat only until you are no longer hungry. No longer being hungry is *not* the same as eating until you have to unbutton your pants and take a nap.

Mindful Eating

Canada's Food Guide encourages us to be mindful of our eating habits. We should eat with others when we can, cook meals at home when possible, and focusing on our meal and the interactions around us.

An example of not being mindful is eating while watching TV or answering emails. Focusing on the experience of the food itself, actually looking at the bite of food, then chewing it thoroughly and savouring the taste and texture, help us to eat more mindfully. These strategies also help prevent us from eating too fast and then overeating.

Professionals often find themselves without the luxury of a lunch break. Therefore, many of them master the ability to eat in record time, quickly consuming food during lulls between appointments.

However, this hurried approach isn't ideal. We will further explore the benefits of slowing down and savouring our meals even amidst a busy day.

My colleagues in the mental health field often end their sessions on mindfulness by taking the participants on silent retreats into nature. They tell me what an incredible experience it is to notice your foot striking the path, listen to the sounds around you as you hike, and feel the wind on your face. Afterward they sit together and have a silent lunch, which can sound so dreamy and foreign to me! They are able to enjoy their surroundings and company without feeling the pressure to fill in the silence. They savour each bite of food and consume it slowly until they are no longer hungry.

This is on a list of things I would love to try one day soon. How about you?

Some of us carry cell phones around like a shield. If we feel socially uncomfortable, we can pull out our phone for a distraction or to avoid interaction. I make a conscious effort to put my phone down, even placing it away from me when I can. This makes my meals and social interactions so much more satisfying.

By minimizing the use of electronics during mealtime, we create space for genuine conversations and deeper connections. The simple act of disconnecting can lead to a more enriching and enjoyable dining experience.

A Mindful Snack

I once came across a useful acronym for better understanding the strategies to enjoying food more mindfully. When you feel stressed or overwhelmed, or when you want a moment of calm awareness, reach for this acronym: SNACK.

- **S**top. Stop what you're doing.
- **N**otice. Notice what's happening within and around you.
- **A**ccept. Acknowledge what's happening without judgment.
- **C**urious. Ground yourself with questions about what's happening with you.
- **K**indness. Respond to yourself and others with kindness.[26]

---

[26] Carla Naumburg, "How to Take a Mindful S.N.A.C.K. Moment," *Mindful.org*. November 18, 2016 (https://www.mindful.org/how-to-take-mindful-snack).

NINE: NUTRITION

STUDY GUIDE QUESTIONS

1. Describe the three sections of the plate according to Canada's Food Guide. Create one breakfast, one lunch, and one dinner meal using the plate method.

2. What are three benefits to eating nutritiously?

3. Grab a packaged food from the pantry and read the label. Are there any hidden sugars? Is it a source of protein? Fiber?

4. List five of your favourite nutritious snack ideas.

Ten

GUT MICROBIOME

THE MORE I learn about the human body and how intricately and brilliantly it was created, the more I praise God.

There are trillions of microorganisms living in our digestive tracts, affecting our overall health. I never imagined that these tiny organisms could impact my immune system, mood regulation, digestion, or risk of developing disease, but there is so much literature tying the wellness of our gut health to our overall well-being.

How Our Gut Affects Overall Health

I have learned that my lifestyle choices, such as diet, habits, and environment, can significantly affect my gut microbiota. I've realized that if I want to maintain a healthy gut, I have to pay attention to these factors. A balanced diet with whole foods, effective meal timing, and appropriate food preparation contributes to gut health.

I noticed that when I was stressed or going through a particularly difficult grieving period, the harmful microbes in my gut seemed to increase, giving rise to all kinds of uncomfortable symptoms. The connection between my mental health and my gut health was a revelation to me, reminding me of the importance of taking care of my body and mind simultaneously, as they are intertwined.

When I began prioritizing my gut health, I noticed improvements in my digestion, energy levels, and mood. I also found that my immune system was stronger and I experienced fewer colds.

The vagus nerve that helps us with relaxation runs through the throat, diaphragm, and gut. Therefore, taking care of our gut health can directly relate to turning off our fight-or-flight response, which is triggered in moments of stress.

How to Care for Your Gut Health

In an effort to make conscious dietary choices, I began incorporating more whole foods, such as fruits, vegetables, whole grains, and lean proteins. I also made an effort to include probiotics, like kefir and fermented foods, to support the good bacteria in my gut. I also really enjoy sauerkraut and miso.

To further support my gut health, I decided to incorporate prebiotics, which provide nourishment for probiotics. Some prebiotic food sources include onions, garlic, leeks, pears, and apples. By consuming these prebiotics alongside probiotics, we aim to create an ideal environment for a diverse and healthy gut microbiome.

I also experimented with different food preparation methods, such as cooking versus consuming raw foods, to find what worked best for me and my digestive system.

I was amazed to learn that a high-fibre diet can increase the diversity of microbes in our guts significantly! This was a great reminder of the importance of getting enough fibre-rich foods such as broccoli, beans, berries, and nuts.

It turns out that taking care of my gut health nourishes not only my body but also my mind and spirit.

TEN: GUT MICROBIOME

STUDY GUIDE QUESTIONS

1. Have you ever gone through a stressful period when you noticed gut health symptoms such as gas, bloating, and reflux?

2. How did God carry you through this event?

3. What prebiotic and probiotic foods would you like to add to your diet?

Eleven

SELF-CARE

FOR A SINGLE mom with two children and a full-time job, self-care was initially the furthest thing from my mind. I was chronically exhausted, emotionally and physically, and barely had time to go to the washroom. Self-care seemed like a really nice but impractical dream.

I eventually learned what mental health professionals have always known and advocated: self-care is not a luxury; it is a necessity.

Indeed, self-care is a cornerstone of optimal wellness. It can be applied to all facets of life—mentally, emotionally, spiritually, and physically. It's essential for anyone who wants to keep up with today's ever-changing world while staying healthy in mind and body.

Self-care assists in the following:

- Physical and mental rest and recovery.
- Improving concentration and cognitive function.
- Releasing muscle tension that may be wired into our brains from past events that affect how we think, feel, and experience life in the present. Stress and trauma can be stored in our bodies because we don't process and release it.
- Improving mental health symptoms and preventing burnout.
- Balancing the body's natural chemicals that are released when we're happy and relaxed instead of stressed and nervous.

- Helping us better cope with daily stressors. It is an important tool in the healing of burnout and pain.
- Taking steps to tend to our emotional, mental, and physical health.
- Checking in regularly with ourselves, watching for physical signs of stress and understanding what our bodies are asking for.
- Practicing self-care can reduce stress, improving your immune systems and increasing productivity.

Types of Self-Care

There are three main varieties of self-care: spiritual, physical, and emotional.

Spiritual self-care. This addresses how you nourish your spirit and reconnect with Jesus. My favourite activities include spending time in quiet reflection, Bible reading, studying the Bible, listening to worship music, journaling, and reading devotionals.

Physical self-care. This includes regular exercise, eating nutritious foods, stretching, and other physically relaxing activities such as taking bubble baths and wearing face masks.

Emotional self-care. This involves setting boundaries, practicing self-compassion, saying no to things that cause stress, engaging in positive self-talk, making self-affirmations, and setting up time to connect with those who are close to us.

My Self-Care Journey

Part of evolving and growing into Sandra 2.0 incorporated trying new things. For example, learning Spanish on Duolingo.[27] I also took up a sewing class. I wasn't very good at first, but I really enjoyed it. I even made a stuffed throw pillow and an apron from an adorable pink camouflage print; it had pockets! In addition, I tried taking new dance classes and found them to be joyful and energetic.

---

[27] Duolingo is a free app that makes it easy to learn other languages.

I came to learn and understand all sorts of easy ways to practice self-care. While I couldn't afford the time or cost of going to a spa for a weekend, I learned about the little things I could do, with little to no cost, that would make a difference.

Self-care isn't just about taking bubble baths and indulging in pedicures, although these are both wonderful practices.

One of my close friends always says, "You can't pour from an empty cup." I feel this truth in my very bones. When I exercise, eat well, spend quiet time with Jesus, and practice stillness and self-care, I am able to provide the best version of myself to care for my children. My cup is full.

Self-care involves regularly caring for yourself and building emotional resilience. What sorts of activities fall into the category of self-care? I would include exercise and nutrition, healthy sleeping habits, spending quiet time with Jesus, fellowshipping with supportive friends and family, engaging in meditation or mindfulness to release stress, and making time for hobbies that increase your sense of well-being. I love reading—and hopefully reading this book is a form of self-care for you! You might also love gratitude practices like prayer and daily journaling.

Strategies for Incorporating Daily Self-Care

To make self-care a regular part of your life, try to make certain practices a part of your regular routine. If you're on the go, find a quiet place to sit in stillness so you can stop moving and focus on your breathing and thoughts. I find that saying arrow prayers is very helpful.[28] There is also a helpful prayer, known as the Jesus Prayer, that when said in quiet and stillness can reset my entire perspective: "My Lord Jesus Christ, Son of the living God, have mercy on me, a sinner."

When you take calming breaths and clear your mind, you signal to the brain that you're no longer in fight-or-flight mode. Rather, you are safe and the parasympathetic nervous system can take over.

I first relax all my muscles through a body scan. What is a body scan? You mentally scan your body, starting from head to toe, slowly relaxing every muscle. Our bodies carry a lot of tension, and we intentionally release each muscle group.

Another practice is called progressive muscle relaxation (PMR), whereby you tense and then release every muscle from head to toe. I tend to carry lots of tension in my eyebrows, jaw, and shoulders. I unfurrow, unclench, and roll back to release this tension.

Once the body is relaxed, you can anchor your thoughts to your breath. Deep breathing involves using your diaphragm to take deep breaths and filling your lungs to full capacity. When you inhale deeply, you expand the lungs and belly, then exhale slowly. Done properly, this also helps strengthen the pelvic floor.

While doing this, I meditate on a passage from Job 33:4: *"The Spirit of God has made me, and the breath of the Almighty gives me life."* It's helpful to remind ourselves that our breaths are sustained by the One who breathed life into us. Life can feel overwhelming, but we are never far from the loving God who created us and called us by name.

Here are a number of other suggestions for ways in which you can effectively practice self-care in your daily life:

---

[28] An arrow prayer is a very quick and short prayer that can be sent up to heaven during any situation, like shooting an arrow with prayer. It's a short message to God and can be as simple as saying "Help me, Lord" or "Thank You, Jesus" as you go about life, as opposed to praying more formally at a dedicated time.

ELEVEN: SELF-CARE

- Prioritize sleep and develop a calming nighttime routine.
- Carve out regular quiet time with God to pray or meditate on His Word.
- Regularly eat gut-healthy foods.
- Develop a regular exercise routine.
- Regularly connect with family and friends.
- Set healthy boundaries.
- Aim to get at least ten minutes of fresh air every day, using all your senses to enjoy the world around you.
- Take deep breaths from your diaphragm.

STUDY GUIDE QUESTIONS

1. Is self-care a luxury or a necessity? Please explain.

2. How do you know whether you've been neglecting your spiritual self-care?

3. How do you currently practice spiritual self-care? Is there anything you would like to change?

4. What are some important boundaries you have in place in your life? Is there an area you struggle with?

Twelve

SINGING AND LAUGHING

IF YOU'VE EVER heard me sing, you may be thinking, *Oh dear...* I am one of those people with a lot of heart but not much natural talent. Whether it's a Christmas concert at my children's school, a hymn I love during communion, or a song that plays on the radio while in the car, I will scrunch up my eyes, tilt my head up, open my mouth wide—and sing passionately. Much to the dismay of my children!

No, I don't sing very well. As a child, I was once asked to only lip-synch during the school concert. This was devastating!

Nevertheless, my lack of talent hasn't deterred me from singing and dancing like nobody's watching.

Singing for Your Mental Health

Why am I encouraging you to sing in a book about recovering from loss, especially when I'm clearly not talented or an expert in the field? I'll tell you why. Singing is excellent for your mental health, even if you're not a great singer! It lowers cortisol and relieves stress and tension. Studies show that when you sing, endorphins are released, which lowers stress levels and improves your outlook.[29] How wonderful!

I enjoy reading in the Bible about singing and rejoicing. A good passage is found in Ephesians 5:19: *"singing and making melody in*

---

[29] Jacques Launay and Eiluned Pearce, "Choir Singing Improves Health, Happiness—and Is the Perfect Icebreaker," *The Conversation*. Date of access: June 21, 2023 (https://theconversation.com/choir-singing-improves-health-happiness-and-is-the-perfect-icebreaker-47619).

your heart to the Lord..." Singing is often celebrated as a way for us to unite in praise of God while nurturing the soul.

Laughing for Your Mental Health
Similarly, laughing is very therapeutic. Here's the fascinating thing: it doesn't have to be authentic laughter for you to reap the benefits!

While at a medical conference, I rushed from one session to the next—and suddenly came to a screeching halt. As I entered one particular hall, instead of encountering soothing slides devoted to the chemical structures of drugs, explanations of evidence-based medicine, and references to peer-reviewed articles, a gentleman on stage was performing a clearly forced laugh and then gesturing for the attendees to reply by copying his laugh in the same tone and volume.

This happened a few more times, and I thought that I must have gone into the wrong room. Then he provided the excellent literature and research supporting what he called "laugh therapy."

Laughter can relieve your stress response, aid in muscle relaxation, and enhance your intake of fresh, oxygenated air, stimulating your organs while releasing endorphins. Studies have shown that laughter can even result in a reduction in pain and an improvement in mood.[30]

Whether you pick up a joke book, watch a funny TV show, or force out a chuckle or two, you can begin experiencing the benefits

---

[30] "Stress Relief from Laughter? It's No Joke," *The Mayo Clinic*. Date of access: June 14, 2023 (https://www.mayoclinic.org/healthy-lifestyle/stress-management/in-depth/stress-relief/art-20044456).

TWELVE: SINGING AND LAUGHING

of laugh therapy. If you need a little encouragement, I have so many cheesy jokes I would love to share with you. Are you ready for one?

Okay, here goes: two antennae got married; the wedding was okay; the reception was incredible.

STUDY GUIDE QUESTIONS

1. Does laughter have to be genuine to result in health benefits? How does laughing help with one's health?

2. Make a list of five songs that can bring you closer to Christ. These should be songs you enjoy singing along to.

3. Read Psalm 98:4 and notice that we are encouraged to shout for joy. Have you ever had an experience when you found joy amidst a dark time? What was that like?

Thirteen

GIVE

YOU MAY BE thinking, "Give? Sandra, I can barely take care of myself right now. How on earth can I give to someone else?" Of course, the timing is completely up to you. Whenever you can, know that giving to others, even in very small ways, can shift the focus from your own misery and increase serotonin and dopamine in the brain, which is associated with feeling pleasure and improved mood. Generosity can lower blood pressure and reduce stress.[31]

Pay It Forward

My children once had a swim meet, and when we arrived I accidentally left my car's hazard lights on. You see, I was in a rush to get to the restroom inside the building; I drink a lot of water and subsequently spend a lot of time rushing to restrooms!

We came back to the car after a long and exhausting day, feeling tired and hungry, only to discover that the car battery had died.

We were fortunate that someone who happened to be walking by had jumper cables and gave us a boost. I was so grateful!

"It's no problem," this stranger replied. "Please just pay it forward."

A few weeks later, a young employee at the grocery store dropped a huge tray of pastries. I rushed over to help. This little bit of

---

[31] "Why Giving Is Good for Your Health," *Cleveland Clinic*. Date of access: June 14, 2023 (https://health.clevelandclinic.org/why-giving-is-good-for-your-health).

assistance wasn't much, but I like to think that it was one opportunity to keep the chain of kindness going. I hope this worker continued to show kindness, passing it on to a patron or colleague and that it will just continue indefinitely.

Ways to Help/Give

There are so many ways in which you can help others or give back to the people around you. Here are some suggestions:

- Call someone to check in on them.
- Purchase a coffee or sandwich at a coffee shop and leave it for the staff to give to someone for free.
- Volunteer at the local food bank or drop off food.
- Write a thank-you note to someone.
- Share your knowledge and expertise.
- Donate time, food, clothing, and furniture.
- Help an elderly or disabled neighbour with yard work.
- Bring food to a sick friend.
- Offer to clean or organize at your church or other charitable organization.

If you look for ways to provide random acts of kindness, you'll be amazed at all the opportunities you find. Just pray: "Lord, I don't have much to give, but show me how to serve You with what I do have."

> If you look for ways to provide random acts of kindness, you'll be amazed at all the opportunities you find.

I love the concept of paying it forward. I once came across a video online depicting a "kindness boomerang." It's beautiful and heart-warming, showing how one random act of kindness can be passed from one person to another.

For example, a young boy falls off his skateboard and his books fly to the ground. A construction worker passing by stops and kindly helps the boy to stand and gathers his fallen items. The boy gets up and goes on his way, only to encounter a woman struggling with her grocery bags. He then helps her by carrying the bags, and the chain continues on.[32]

STUDY GUIDE QUESTIONS

1. Proverbs 11:25 says, *"A generous person will prosper; whoever refreshes others will be refreshed"* (NIV). Reflect on this passage and what it means in your day-to-day life.

2. How has giving affected you spiritually?

3. What are some ways in which you can give without spending any money?

4. What are three examples of random acts of kindness?

---

[32] "Life Vest Inside—Kindness Boomerang—'One Day,'" *YouTube*. August 29, 2011 (https://www.youtube.com/watch?v=nwAYpLVyeFU&ab_channel=LifeVestInside).

Fourteen

SLEEP

INSOMNIA IS A common struggle after loss and trauma. For me, it was really tough to sleep following my husband's passing. For several months, I had slept fitfully either at a hospital or at home, jolting awake for frequent updates.

If you've ever struggled with sleep, you probably know that it's very common to start getting stressed about your sleep—and your inability to sleep causes further difficulty in sleeping. It can become a vicious cycle.

Our sleep is so very important, as it affects our mood, productivity, food cravings, immune system, and even our ability to build muscle.

> Our sleep is so very important, as it affects our mood, productivity, food cravings, immune system, and even our ability to build muscle.

For myself and other widows I've spoken with, nighttime can be particularly challenging. Perhaps your story is like mine and you tried to outrun your pain only for it to all come crashing down when you finally slowed down a little. Or maybe your house just feels uncomfortably quiet and you can't bear to walk by your partner's things or look at their side of the bed. If so, I know it's hard and I'm sending you lots of love and prayers.

I work with many patients to help them practice good sleep hygiene. They learn strategies to improve their sleep, and these are all strategies that I've put to the test myself when my own life was flipped upside-down. I would like to share some of these strategies with you.

Consider the timing of your meals. Eat balanced meals during the day and complete your meals at least three hours before bed. This can help to improve your sleep.

Stay hydrated. Drinking water frequently throughout the day has many health benefits. Minimize fluid intake in the evening to limit nocturnal awakenings to use the washroom.

Exercise regularly. Regular exercise is valuable in terms of increasing your sleep quality. However, exercise that happens within three hours of bedtime may increase your core body temperature and make it more difficult to fall asleep.

Watch your caffeine and alcohol intake. Limiting your caffeine consumption after noon and minimizing your overall consumption of alcohol can improve your sleep quality.

Wind down one hour before bed. This will be tremendously helpful in restoring your sleep. Consider this your "protected time" before bed, a time reserved for relaxing, restorative self-care activities that don't involve any electronic devices. You should put away your devices and not touch them again until morning.

You may be scratching your head and wondering what you should do without any electronics. I invite you to think of a calming activity you may have engaged in before your life got so busy. Or is there something you've always wanted to do but haven't had the time to pursue?

Develop a calming and soothing bedtime routine. Listening to calm nature sounds or soothing music, doing gentle stretches, sitting in stillness, and practicing deep breathing can help with relaxation. Consider taking a relaxing bubble bath or lighting some candles. Enjoy a cup of herbal tea under a cozy blanket. Reading a book or magazine can distract you without being overstimulating. Just choose your book wisely. Ideally, avoid cliffhangers or high suspense.

Other activities such as crossword puzzles, word searches, sudoku, puzzles, colouring, painting, knitting, prayer, crocheting, or model-building can be popular ways to wind down at night.

Manage your thoughts. If thoughts of sadness or worry start to creep in, you can gently acknowledge them and then let them roll on by without inviting them to pull up a chair and stay. This is a powerful time for spiritual self-care. As you focus on Jesus, everything else will fall into place. I have a relaxing playlist of hymns and songs that I enjoy listening to. I can close my eyes, breathe deeply, and meditate.

If you're having ruminative thoughts, or too many thoughts, when trying to settle down, consider finding time earlier in the day to write them down. Write about these worries and include solutions for each, if available. This simple act of "downloading" the thoughts onto paper can be helpful in terms of clearing the mind.

After this, take the paper and put it aside, knowing that you've done what you can about the day's issues. This may help you to relax and focus your mind on other things.

Go to bed only when you're sleepy. It's also a good idea to only go to bed when you're sleepy. It's important that these nighttime activities be done out of the bed. Avoid getting into bed too early, so that your brain can associate the bed with the act of sleeping.

Get up and try again. If you're awake in bed for more than twenty minutes or so, the recommendation is to get out of bed, once again do a relaxing activity, and then try again once you're sleepy.[33] Again, this helps to re-establish the brain connection that the bed is for sleeping.

Have a fixed wake-up time. Maintain a fixed wake-up time, seven days per week, to reset your circadian rhythm (body clock), and avoid naps as much as possible. This may be a work in progress.

Consider trying meditation apps or software to guide you through deep breathing.[34] I also really enjoy playing worship songs

---

[33] Just don't be a clock-watcher, which can cause more anxiety about the inability to sleep.

[34] Some options include Insight Timer, Headspace, and Calm.

and meditating on peaceful words of faith. This can calm the mind and create a serene environment for sleep.

Consume sleep-friendly foods for dinner as much as you can. This includes fatty fish, walnuts, pistachios, sour cherries, and yogurt, all of which contain melatonin.

Don't be too hard on yourself if you struggle with these sleep hygiene strategies. Just do what you can to attain deep, restorative sleep. Know that prioritizing sleep and self-care will be an important part of your wellness journey.

STUDY GUIDE QUESTIONS

1. What are some spiritual activities you can incorporate in your one hour of winddown time before bed?

2. What are three non-electronic activities you can do in the evenings?

3. What are the impacts of exercise, caffeine intake, and electronics use on your sleep? How can you mitigate their interference?

4. What are two sleep-friendly foods?

Fifteen

HEALING AND TRIGGERS

I USED TO think of healing as a destination: "I will fully heal and then start my life again." However, I've learned that healing is an ongoing journey.

You cannot find peace by avoiding life. Nobody can tell you how long it will take to reach a point where the pain you feel no longer overshadows everything else. Prayer, self-care, and the wellness strategies we've already discussed can support you on your journey.

Triggers

It can be helpful to be prepared for triggers and anticipate them when possible. Even eight years later, I'm still occasionally ambushed by a painful trigger. However, it's rarer now and I am able to withstand the pain with greater strength and God's grace. I allow myself to feel, to mourn, and to move forward.

During the first year, the biggest triggers for me were all the firsts. The first anniversary, the first birthday, and the first holidays may be the most difficult. Subsequent years will often be easier. The key is to prepare yourself and decide ahead of time whether you would like to change certain traditions or patterns. Do what feels right for you—and your children, if you have them.

For example, Christmas was a big holiday for us and we had a whole routine that spanned the holidays. That first year, I couldn't even bear the thought of putting up a Christmas tree or decorating the house.

I did, however, want to do something joyful for the children, so we did something nontraditional, and it was the best thing for us that year. With my parents, we stayed over at a hotel and waterpark for a few days. They had fun in the daytime, there were Christmas decorations, and we attended the service at a nearby church where I didn't know a single person, nor did they know me or my circumstances. For me, that's exactly what I needed that year.

In subsequent years, with God's grace, we were able to rejoin our community and families and make new traditions. In my humble opinion, being prepared and thinking of fun ideas to change patterns can be helpful.

When I work with a patient who's trying to make a significant life change, such as quit smoking, one of the first things we do is change some existing patterns. If you try to do your exact same routine minus the cigarette, the absence will be glaring and challenging. If you change your routine, however, it can feel easier.

I've seen this happen time and time again. A patient who always has coffee and a cigarette first thing in the morning may instead wake up and go for a walk, drink water, then have coffee at work. That makes it easier to eliminate the morning cigarette, even though that's often the most difficult time of the day.

I believe it to be similar with loss. I left my husband's possessions for as long as I needed to—I don't actually remember how long—because putting them away was too painful. I listened to my feelings.

However, preserving these items and seeing them around just as I always had, as if he was going to come home one of these days, was also painful. Once I was able to put things away and create my own routine and use the space in our home differently, some of that pain lifted.

Certain triggers can't be prepared for, and that's okay. However, understanding why this happens and how you can manage it may

FIFTEEN: HEALING AND TRIGGERS

help. Know that you may be challenged and triggered from time to time, but you're going to be able to handle it. Counselling can be a tremendous help.

An example of an unexpected trigger happened when my children and I attended a birthday party several months after our loss. In my mind, things were going relatively well. My days were less terrible and I was incorporating some of the wellness strategies we've already discussed in this book.

Out of nowhere, though, my son came up to me with such a sweet and heartbroken look on his face and asked, "Mom, why did Dad have to die? I want to go on his shoulders like the other kids are on their dads' shoulders."

In that moment, I felt my heart break open even wider than it had before. Despite all my attempts to be both Mom and Dad and provide what I could for the kids, sometimes we came up against the hard reality that I still wasn't Dad.

I cuddled my son and I empathized with him, and he eventually ran off and laughed and played. I was wrecked.

Knowing that my brain's smoke alarm, the amygdala, was blaring *Danger*, I was able to do my best to calm my emotions. I stepped away, slowed my breathing, and drank some water. I said a prayer and eventually was able to rejoin the party.

How Others Respond to You

Once I made the decision to start living again, my perspective changed. I started to gain confidence in my faith and in my walk with Christ. I started to have hope for the future and contribute to how I wanted that future to look like.

What I didn't anticipate was that some people weren't going to be happy for me. So ground yourself in God and use that connection with Him to guide your reaction when people respond to you and your wellness journey.

EMBRACING ABUNDANCE

Those closest to me were incredible. I'm so thankful for my parents, siblings, in-laws, and friends. They carried my children and me, hugged, us, exercised and played with us, and prayed with us and for us. I love them so much.

Not everyone was so kind. I would get the odd snarky remark, clothed in saccharine sweetness: "Oh, you're not wearing black for the whole year? Why not?" "Wow, you must be really strong. If it was me, I would just lay at home crying. But look at you, all out and about." When you're already barely holding it together, it's hard to deal with these ambushes and judgments.

This reminds me of another famous saying I really love, and I think you will too: "Be who you are and say what you mean. Those who matter don't mind and those who mind don't matter."

> **God is love. Therefore, any comment that isn't born of love is not of Christ.**

Remember that when people are snarky and judgmental, it's not coming from God. God is love. Therefore, any comment that isn't born of love is not of Christ. Continue with your faith, your spiritual advisor, and those who love you—and be strong. You are a new version of yourself and stronger than you could ever imagine.

The really great thing is that you don't have to be strong. I wasn't strong at all. I don't say this with false humility; I'm telling you the full honest to God truth. I was a mess. A complete mess.

Jesus carried me. I couldn't have moved off the metaphorical broken glass I was lying in without laying it all on Jesus, who said, *"Come to Me, all you who labor and are heavy laden, and I will give you rest"* (Matthew 11:28). I took Jesus up on that offer, and He still carries me every day of my life.

For someone who works so hard on building her physical strength and mental well-being, it was incredibly humbling to be brought so low. However, in my weakness He truly showed me His strength.

Thank You, Jesus!

FIFTEEN: HEALING AND TRIGGERS

I know that He wants to carry you too, my friend. Please invite Him to do so and draw near to Him.

Let's remember that God asks us not to judge one another, but rather to love one another. If a widow wants to wear bright clothing or attend a gathering where she tries to smile and enjoy herself, please don't judge her or make her feel bad. It's cruel and not what Jesus would do. How a widow or widower handles their grief in manner, in attire, or in attendance is in no way a certain reflection of the love and respect they had for the person who has passed. It is simply that they are trying hard to create a new normal and reinvent their lives. You can have loved your spouse very much, have infinite respect for them and their family, and still choose to live the life that God has gifted you.

It takes some time to reinvent yourself, so be patient and be kind with yourself in the process. Know that of all your identities the one that is most important can never be stripped away: you are the daughter or son of the Most High. Adjust your crown and know that you are cherished. God has you.

STUDY GUIDE QUESTIONS

1. Are there any triggers in your life that remind you of a painful time? How can you lean in to Jesus when you feel triggered?

2. What lies is the enemy spinning about this trigger and what does Jesus say about it?

3. What are some safeguards or strategies you use when you feel triggered?

IN THE NEXT four chapters, I will continue to share my personal story of healing and living abundantly with God's grace. These chapters have some content that may be particularly relevant to those who have lost a spouse through death or divorce. We will explore topics such as navigating relationships with former in-laws, moving forward after a loss, venturing back into the dating world, and discerning Jesus's voice. I will also share my personal journey with dating after loss and remarriage.

I invite you to join me on this ongoing journey, but be aware that all of this content may not be directly applicable to your own situation. I believe that within these chapters you will still find insights and perspectives that resonate with you.

Let's continue together and may God reveal valuable insights for you to discover.

Sixteen

FORMER IN-LAWS

I AM THANKFUL that my late husband's family was, and continues to be, loving and supportive. They were respectful of the distance I needed in order to grieve, understanding that everyone grieves differently. My deep connection and love for them continues to this day, but I had a really hard time seeing them during my grief because they were such a reminder to me of who was missing in my life. I'm sure it was the same for them.

However, as time passed, efforts were made on both sides to continue to consider each other as family. I am grateful for them and thankful that they are such an essential source of love and joy in our lives.

From speaking with other widows, I know that in-law relationships don't always go this way. There are many factors in play, including what the relationship was like before the loss, how seeing each other makes everyone feel, and whether boundaries are respected. Some widows have faced rejection, hostility, and stress from their former in-laws. Death can bring out the absolute worst in some people, and the former in-law relationship can be tricky to navigate.

If your experience has been different or painful, I encourage you to pray about it and place boundaries where they are needed. Speaking to a skilled counsellor may also help put things in perspective and help navigate this complex relationship.

You deserve respect, understanding, and support during this difficult time. Surround yourself with those who cherish and uplift you as you continue to navigate your wellness journey.

STUDY GUIDE QUESTIONS

1. Are there any people in your life who are part of a former version of yourself?

2. What are some boundaries you can put in place?

Seventeen

MOVING FORWARD

MOVING FORWARD AFTER a loss doesn't mean that you forget the past. It means acknowledging your pain and using it to promote growth and resilience. With Jesus, the support of your loved ones, and the strength that lies within you, you have the power to reinvent yourself. Embrace the process and trust yourself.

Focus on your purpose and finding things you love. Continue to practice self-care. When you're feeling up to it, consider personal growth. Is there a course you always wanted to take? A hobby you wanted to pursue? Perhaps you could take on photography, cross-weaving, sewing, pottery, boxing, or learn a new language.

There's an old business saying that says, "Anything that doesn't continue to grow is dead." Is this not true for us as well?

Moving Forward

I'm a naturally outgoing and friendly person, but reintegrating into society was frightening for me. I managed it by taking baby steps.

I would arrive at my group fitness class just as it started and bolt out again right afterwards. This helped to keep socializing to a minimum.

However, as a few weeks passed, I gradually found that greeting people and engaging in some small talk was enjoyable. It wasn't the frightening task I had pegged it to be.

Once you've watered your soul and body, consider tentatively stretching out and branching into new areas. Remember that you are reinventing a stronger and more resilient version of yourself, with God's grace.

Also, when you take a class or undertake a new activity, whether it's at the community centre, gym or a studio, you will also be spreading your wings a little. Start to slowly reconnect with the outside world and others.

STUDY GUIDE QUESTIONS

1. In what ways do you feel stuck in your current circumstances?

2. How would you like to move forward in your life?

3. Are there any biblical truths about your identity that you can hold on to? For example, *"I am fearfully and wonderfully made"* (Psalm 139:14, NIV) and *"For I know the plans I have for you... plans to prosper you and not to harm you, plans to give you hope and a future'"* (Jeremiah 29:11, NIV).

Eighteen

DATING

HOW DO YOU know when you're ready to start dating after loss? My own journey taught me some important truths.

For example, I thought I was ready to date when I actually wasn't. You know what they say: hindsight is 20/20. I felt so lonely and incomplete. I very much wanted a partner and a father figure for my children. What I learned later is that these weren't the right reasons for me to start dating. I wasn't yet content in who I was. I didn't yet feel whole and secure in my identity.

I fumbled through online dating, and it certainly was eye-opening. Whether you consider online dating or not is a personal choice, although I'm happy to share my experience with you if it may shed some light on the avenues available to you.

Online dating hadn't been around when I was younger, so I found the whole process to be very curious. There were free apps, as well as ones with paid subscriptions. Some used algorithms and others catered to certain faiths and cultures.

Considering that I wasn't going out much, it seemed like an interesting way to meet people. I enjoyed being able to set criteria, preselecting geography, religion, education, age, and openness to having kids.

There were also apps where only women could initiate contact. In others, the app would make the matches. In some, you could swipe left (no) or right (yes), and your phone would give a celebratory ping if you had both swiped right.

I quickly learned from those around me that some apps were used for casual meetups and others were intended for the more marriage-minded.

There are important safety tips to keep in mind, such as never sharing personal details, addresses, phone numbers, or banking information. If a couple decides to progress from online chats to phone calls, some apps facilitate ways to have a video or phone chat in the app itself without the need for either person to share their personal phone number or contact details.

If by some chance you found someone you eventually wanted to meet in public, the best approach was to choose a very public place during the daytime and let others know where you would be, with whom, and when.

Another important tip: beware of catfishing! This is when someone uses a fake persona and name to lure people in.

Short of catfishing, some people use embellishments or provide very outdated photos—for example, showing them to be twenty years younger and twenty pounds lighter.

You may feel some initial excitement about a Christian you come across. However, you may find that when you ask about his faith, it isn't really an important part of his life. He may be a Christian in name only.

While I met some wonderful people and found that it helped me to socialize again, in the end I found that online dating wasn't for me.

By the time I really was ready, many years after I had initially thought I was, I felt more content with my circumstances. I wasn't living the life I wanted by any stretch of the imagination, but I was learning to love it. I didn't even cringe at the word *widow* anymore. Big leaps indeed! I had accepted and even embraced my new reality. From time to time, I would think to myself, *It's nice being single! I'm my own solid unit. I'm rocking this as best I can.*

EIGHTEEN: DATING

When I reached that pivotal state of being content in my circumstances, I started to pray for my very own Boaz, from the story of Ruth. If it was God's will for me to remarry, and if I met a godly man who would love me and my children as Christ loves the church, I would consider it.

I was going to be just fine if God didn't send me a Boaz.

Quick question for you: what was Boaz before he met Ruth? Ruthless! Sorry, I can't help myself.

One day, a good friend came over and told me about a really great guy at her church who made their *orban*, a kind of holy bread used in the divine liturgy.[35] She showed me a photo of this man and his son at a children's event, dressed in their church tunics. He was demonstrating how to make the holy bread, and there on the mantle behind him was a photo of the Virgin Mary smiling. I felt her presence.

From that photograph, I had no idea how much I would come to love the man and his son.

My friend asked if it would be okay for her to connect us.

"Sure," I said.

Meanwhile, she messaged him to ask the same. He replied: "Thanks. I am going to pray about it and then give her a call."

She and I both happily sighed over this lovely response.

By the third day, he still hadn't sent a message. I began to wonder if "I am going to pray about it" was actually code for "I find her unattractive."

In any case, after about three days, he did send a message — and the journey that unfolded has been a great blessing in our lives. We married and began our shared journey as a blended and blessed family.

It turned out that he and I had been friends in Sunday school as young children. We'd had the same Father of Confession throughout

---

[35] The following words are inscribed on the blessed loaf of round bread: *Agios Otheos, Agios Esheros, Agios Athanatos.* Meaning: "Holy God, Holy Mighty, Holy Immortal."

our entire lives and our parents were friends who attended the same liturgy.

We cautiously and slowly became friends while seeking guidance from our spiritual Father. I can't stress enough how important it is to pray for and with each other when you're trying to determine if the person you're considering is part of God's plan for your life.

I will share the steps I have used, but remember: the Holy Spirit doesn't rush. I encourage you to take things very slow when getting to know someone. Frequently ask yourself whether the relationship is pulling you closer or pushing you away from Jesus. As two people draw close to Jesus, they also draw close to one another.

If you do remarry, I pray that you become a strand of three with Jesus. As Ecclesiastes 4:12 tells us, *"A threefold cord is not quickly broken."*

First, find out who you are in your singleness, and know that this is where you are meant to be in this time. What does God want you to learn in this season? How can you lean into Him?

I recently read a wonderful book called *Whatever, God* by Father Anthony Messeh. It was such a great read! Its focus is on how we completely surrender our lives to Jesus by telling Him we will do whatever He calls us to do.[36]

Whether or not you choose to remarry, you can honour your future spouse by keeping God above all and before all. When God is in His rightful place in our lives, we will naturally honour our future spouse.

What happens if you're struggling during the period of waiting? I know that it's tough not knowing what shape your life will take. However, remember that we trust God and His infinite wisdom and perfect timing. Know that He is working during the wait—on your story and on you. Try to focus on not getting stuck while waiting because you don't know which way to go. Consider self-growth and

---

[36] Father Anthony Messeh, *Whatever, God* (Maitland, FL: Xulon Press, 2017).

exploration. Hobbies, friendships, and service, for example, are ways in which you can continue to thrive in life.

For the times when you're lonely and missing physical intimacy, a passage from 1 Thessalonians 4:3–4 comes to mind: *"For this is the will of God, your sanctification: that you should abstain from sexual immorality; that each of you should know how to possess his own vessel in sanctification and honor..."*

Purity is how we are called to live. Research has reported that couples who have sex within marriage report higher relationship stability and satisfaction, better sexual quality, and better communication.[37] Let us strive to be pure in heart, thought, and action. As Matthew 5:8 tells us, *"Blessed are the pure in heart, for they shall see God."*

Another thing to keep in mind is this: when interested gentlemen come out of the woodwork, don't sell yourself short. I've spoken to widows who felt like they're a burden with lots of baggage; they don't think anyone would be willing to take that on. Therefore, they're grateful when any suitor comes around.

This simply isn't true. Yes, you have endured some terrible pain, and it may have inflicted some emotional wounds. You can heal, you can be whole, and you are going to be an incredible partner to the anointed spouse God chooses for you, if that is His will.

So please do not settle for the first person who comes your way just because you feel grateful. If he is the one God has sent, you will have peace.

---

[37] Dr. Andrew Magers, "The Science of Sex Before Marriage," *The Well Clinic*. February 20, 2020 (https://mywellclinic.com/blog/2020/02/20/science-sex-marriage).

STUDY GUIDE QUESTIONS

1. How can you be comforted and encouraging during your season of waiting?

2. What do the Bible and current research tell us about the benefits of purity outside of marriage?

3. How does drawing close to God bring us closer to our partners?

Nineteen

HOW TO KNOW IF SOMETHING COMES FROM JESUS

IN THIS WELLNESS journey, one of the deepest desires of the heart is to hear the voice of Jesus and understand His will for our lives. I often read about this. Here are some steps that I have found helpful while seeking to know whether something in my life comes from God.

We will begin with seven questions to discern God's will for your life.

- Will your choice glorify God?
- Does your choice align with the Word of God?
- Do you feel at peace with this choice?
- Does the Holy Spirit confirm your decision?
- Does your decision continue to hold true and feel right over time?
- Will your decision align with spiritual guidance you receive?
- Have you surrendered the decision to God and asked for wisdom discernment?

In James 1:5, we encounter one of the most comforting verses in the Bible: *"If any of you lacks wisdom, let him ask of God, who gives to all liberally and without reproach, and it will be given to him."*

I often need wisdom and discernment in my life. Especially as a widow, I struggled in the early days of managing the uncharted territory I was passing through. For example, how could I support my children on Father's Day?

Considerations for Remarriage

Suppose you find yourself in a godly relationship that is heading towards marriage. You have taken it slowly and reviewed all the above parameters. Your spiritual advisor and closest friends and family are at peace with this individual. You believe this person cares for you—and your children, if you have them—as Jesus cares for the church. Now you are planning for a wedding!

Here are some important thoughts for your consideration.

Do not compare your current partner and relationship to your former spouse and former marriage. You aren't the same person you were then, and your new spouse is their own unique person. It's very important not to compare each other to prior spouses. Instead forge your own path and dynamic with both of you and Jesus.

Your late spouse's family and friends may initially struggle with seeing you with someone else. Be kind and respect their feelings. If they don't want to celebrate your relationship, or if they pull back from you, respect their boundaries. Everyone navigates pain differently. You will also set your own boundaries for them to respect. You may find that people have mixed reactions, with some being incredibly happy for you and others being uncomfortable. That's okay. You aren't doing anything wrong, and acceptance can take time.

Traditional marriage counselling is great and I highly recommend it. I particularly appreciate the Prepare/Enrich program that you as a couple can review with your spiritual advisor or counsellor. It asks each individual a long list of questions about a variety of topics and then prepares a report which underlines strong and weak areas of your relationship.

Also, bear in mind that there are so many new things to learn as part of a blended family. I struggled to find resources in this area—that is, until I came across an incredibly helpful program called Blended and Blessed. My partner and I attended a virtual session with Ron Deal, an expert on blended families and author of *The Smart Stepfamily* books, and Gary Chapman, who pioneered the concept of the five love languages. You will also be able to find resources online, including helpful podcasts and articles.

With blended families, there are so many considerations. For example, how long does it take for a family to blend? The truth is that these families aren't assembled in blenders, but rather slow-cookers. It can take anywhere from three to five years, but families may vary in terms of the time they need to blend. This is so helpful to know!

Other areas that may need attention are tips related to how to discipline biological children versus stepchildren, how to build bonds, how to manage interactions with ex-spouses, etc. These areas are so much easier to navigate with the help of amazing resources.

Documents to Consider for Remarriage

It is also highly recommended that you speak with a lawyer well before the wedding date to discuss any financial, legal, guardianship considerations, or other suggestions. I will mention two here, but this is by no means comprehensive. I encourage you to speak with a legal expert.

Pre-marriage contract. If you're remarrying and have children, a pre-marriage contract is highly recommended. This should be done well before the wedding, as may be invalidated if there is later any concern that one party felt rushed.

Wills and estate planning. Any previous wills you may have had are no longer valid once you remarry. It is strongly recommended to draft new wills, especially if you have children or are bringing new assets or debt into the marriage.

STUDY GUIDE QUESTIONS

1. Describe the steps that can help you to determine whether something comes from Jesus.

2. Do you have a spiritual mentor? If not, is there someone you can consider for this role in your life?

3. James 1:5 says, *"If any of you lacks wisdom, let him ask of God, who gives to all liberally and without reproach, and it will be given to him."* What are you praying about today that you would like wisdom and discernment for?

CONCLUSION

DEAR FRIEND, I know that you've suffered loss and that you feel pain. I'm sorry for your pain, and I'm sorry that you are hurting. You will have to take it one day at a time.

My experience is just one experience. Every single one of us will have some differences, and maybe some similarities, along our own individual path.

Regardless of what you have endured, you may feel that your identity has changed. As you go on this adventure of reinventing your new life and identity, remember that first and foremost you are the child of the King.

God has plans to prosper you and not to harm you, plans for hope and a future. You can choose to live the life you have and live it abundantly. You can choose to start taking baby steps to improve the quality of your spiritual life, and your physical and mental fitness.

I have no doubt, not even one, that if you choose today to surrender your life into God's loving and very capable hands, you will be amazed at where your life will go. May your departed loved ones be honoured and forever remembered. May you continue to heal and continue to grow.

Let's make a big effort to help others. You will soon be able to support someone new to trauma and loss, and I pray that you will share all that you have learned so that we can continue to carry and love one another.

ABOUT THE AUTHOR

SANDRA TADROS GUIRGUIS is a passionate Orthodox Christian, dedicated wife, and loving mother of three children. She resides in Toronto, Canada where she has built a fulfilling career as a healthcare professional, fitness expert, and public/corporate speaker.

Sandra works with patients and clients to improve their sleep, eating habits, and physical activity. She also assists those living with chronic diseases and helps them to thrive.

As a public wellness speaker, Sandra inspires others to live abundantly and find joy in their everyday lives. She is a sought-after youth and young adult speaker, encouraging them to live their best lives in service to Jesus. She is a strong advocate for mental health awareness and support, using her platform to break down barriers and foster open conversations.

In her free time, she enjoys reading, baking, exercising, and engaging in spirited boardgame sessions with her family. She is the proud owner of STG Wellness, which has been featured in prominent lifestyle magazines.

Having navigated the difficult journey of grief, Sandra connects with others who have experienced loss, offering her support and guidance along the way.

This, her debut book, is a culmination of her experiences, expertise, and deep-rooted faith. It serves as a comprehensive guide to wellness, covering topics such as identity, grief support, children, and various aspects of wellness, including stress management, relationships, meditation, mindfulness, exercise, nutrition, gut health, and self-care. In this heartfelt and practical resource, Sandra also shares her perspectives on healing, triggers, moving forward, dating, and discerning Jesus's will in one's life.

With a dedication to Jesus at the core of her work, Sandra embarks on this new journey as an author, inviting readers to join her in the pursuit of a well-rounded, abundant life rooted in faith, wellness, and love.

www.ingramcontent.com/pod-product-compliance
Lightning Source LLC
Chambersburg PA
CBHW031121080526
44587CB00011B/1059